The eBay
Business Handbook

How Anyone Can Build a Business
and Make Money on eBay

Robert Pugh

Hh Harriman House Publishing

HARRIMAN HOUSE LTD

3A Penns Road
Petersfield
Hampshire
GU32 2EW
GREAT BRITAIN

Tel: +44 (0)1730 233870
Fax: +44 (0)1730 233880
Email: enquiries@harriman-house.com
Website: www.harriman-house.com

First published in Great Britain in 2006
Reprinted 2007
Copyright © Harriman House Ltd

The right of Robert Pugh to be identified as Author has been asserted in
accordance with the Copyright, Design and Patents Act 1988.

ISBN: 1-8975-9768-1
ISBN 13: 978-1897597-68-2

British Library Cataloguing in Publication Data
A CIP catalogue record for this book can be obtained from the British
Library.

Printed and bound by Biddles Ltd, Kings Lynn, Norfolk.

Contents

Sign up to the FREE eBay UK Bulletin

If this book has helped you with your eBay business and you would like to know more, why not sign up for my weekly newsletter and keep up-to-date with the latest developments for eBay sellers. You can also send me your feedback and tell me how this book has kick-started your eBay adventure.

Distributed by the publisher of this book – Harriman House – each e-mail contains hints and tips for eBay sellers, technical developments within eBay, a reader's letter ('Ask Molly') and other essential information. HTML issues are also covered, with explanations of when and how to use additional codes to drive your profits even higher. Plus, check out new ideas surrounding general sales techniques and advice for moving with the markets.

It's not all hard work and no play. There are always strange and crazy things happening on eBay and in my 'Trader's Tales' section, I will share some of the more amusing moments from the world of sales. Like the guy who bought 'half a kilo of Lego' and then was disappointed with the amount! Not to mention the weird and wonderful auctions that take place online - how much would you bid for an 'air guitar'?

You can also keep up-to-date with my own eBay career; I'll share my experiences, both good and bad, with you.

To sign up to my free newsletter, please visit: www.ebaybulletin.co.uk

Best wishes,

Bob (Mollybol)

About the author

After 24 years working for the same company, and many years within the corporate sales division, Bob realised it was time for a change.

He began selling on eBay in January 2003, initially by clearing his house of unwanted items, with very little knowledge of computers and no experience of selling via the internet. The first few months proved to be a steep learning curve, but he soon became an established eBay Power Seller and has sold over 9,000 items.

Now, aged 41, he has retired from full-time work and uses eBay to generate an income as and when it is required.

Since this book was first published, Bob has made numerous radio appearances to share his expert eBay knowledge and has received plenty of positive feedback:

"As eBay is now a part of life, we were very privileged to broadcast a programme about it. It's changed people's lives completely - it's a monster that has grown and grown and has made so much money, for so many people. Bob was so enthusiastic on-air and actually taught me a hell of a lot about eBay - and what a great book he has written too."

- Pete Price, Presenter, *Radio City*

He now writes a free, weekly newsletter - offering tips, advice and real-life stories about the world's most famous online marketplace. Sign up today, at: www.ebaybulletin.co.uk

Preface

This book will take you from the very first act of creating your user name through to the creation of your own business.

The eBay process is very easy; to sell on eBay is not complicated and requires no sales experience. However, to use eBay to it's full potential, to maximise returns and develop a robust online business, does require an understanding of sales, marketing and business processes. It is these thoughts and techniques that can be found within these pages.

Who the book is for

This book has been written for anyone who has ever considered the idea of owning their own business and being their own boss. Whether you want to supplement an existing income, or you want a complete change in life, this book is for you.

The book assumes that the reader already knows the basics about eBay, but no great knowledge of running a business, sales techniques or computers is assumed. These areas are covered within these pages to a depth that will enable you to be successful without becoming bogged down with technical detail.

Written in plain English, this book does not require the reader to have a grasp of complex industry jargon; all that is required is an open mind and a desire to succeed.

This book also contains more advanced ideas for anyone with an existing eBay business. With a fresh, common sense approach to selling, there are many hints, tips and personal recommendations that can be applied to your eBay activities.

This Handbook is intended as an introduction to successful eBay selling for those who would like to know more. It demonstrates how anyone can start in a small way and then grow at their own pace to a level to be decided by themselves.

What the book covers

This book provides you with everything you need to know to get started on eBay as a seller, or improve your sales and profit if you already trade. The book is structured in a logical way, from the most basic planning in the early stages to managing the paperwork.

Unlike other eBay books, this Handbook is based on the personal experiences of an established Power Seller. Everything from the practical concerns of international sales to the purchase of packing materials is covered here.

Perhaps one of the more valuable aspects of this book is the section dedicated to finding stock to sell. Where traders obtain their stock is a closely guarded secret and often finding where to buy can be quite daunting. This book will inform you where to look, how to buy from different sources and, the most interesting of all, how to use eBay as a source of goods.

This book cannot cover every aspect of selling on eBay, there is just not enough space. It will, however, show how I went from zero to 4,000+ feedbacks in just two years. From the very first LP record to the family car, I have sold items into almost every corner of the globe, taken every form of payment known to man, and personally packed a huge variety of items. Anybody can do this, just follow the steps in this book, dedicate the time, set your own goals and soon you will achieve them.

Structure of the book

This book has been structured in such a way that it covers all aspects of creating an eBay business; from the very first idea, through the processes involved, to building your business for the future. The book follows a logical progression that allows you to evolve at your own speed.

The development of an eBay business can be achieved in several stages, and the chapters of the book reflect this.

How to get started

The chapter 'Starting out' covers the thinking required behind an online business prior to actually selling. Areas covered in detail include:

- What eBay is actually all about, how it all began, what kind of things are allowed be sold and what items should be avoided.

- How much is a typical eBay business actually going to cost to get started? This section looks at the practical requirements, a few of the problems you may encounter along the way and gives an idea of just how much time it will take.

- How to choose the items that you want to sell. This section also looks at the best time to sell.

- How to research your chosen market and discover what is really selling, and how your competition is doing. Searching the eBay database is a key element to successful trading – learn how best to use the system to your advantage.

- Creating your seller's account: considering everything from the right name to the format of your auction design, and how to promote your sales activities to achieve maximum return on your investment.

- How big you would like your market to be, whether you should sell overseas and what is really involved.

- How you will trade and what terms and conditions will you include? This section provides practical examples of what to include and why. What will you do regarding your postage conditions, how will you handle any returned goods, and how long will you allow for payment to be made? It's all in this section.

- Understanding which forms of payment option are available. This section is dedicated to this subject and analyses each payment method, providing a comparison between them.

Preparing for the first auction

This chapter looks at all of the preliminary work involved before the first auction goes live.

- Check out the competition; find out what's selling and what is not fetching the right price. See how your chosen item has been selling during the last month.

- Guidelines on how to prepare your item for the auction.

- Advice and guidance on the packing materials you will need, where best to obtain them and how much they will cost.

- Consider how you will post your item, which carrier you will use, how much it is likely to cost, and how best to package your item to ensure a safe delivery.

- Which camera should you buy and how much will it cost? Advice and examples regarding saving your pictures onto your computer and how to edit them. Plus hints and tips for the best pictures.

Creating your first auction

This chapter is a complete step by step walk-through of listing an auction on eBay, with hints and tips at every stage.

- How the mechanics of the process actually work; what you really need to know to sell your first item.

- Ensure you get the maximum number of visitors to see your item by selecting the correct location on eBay to place your auction.

- It's all about choosing the best title in this section. Without a good title, nobody will find your auction in the first place.

- It is the description of your item that will convince the visitor to bid. This section looks in detail at various techniques used for describing your item and shows how to make it look its best.

- What to consider when setting a start price, how long should you allow your auction to run, when should you start it and should you use a reserve? This section also covers the loading of your pictures onto eBay and outlines the extra options available to promote your auction.

- What is likely to happen during the auction, what kind of contact might you get from potential bidders and how to deal with this. You may decide to revise your auction details, cancel bids or even remove the auction altogether. This section covers the processes you will need to know.

When the auction ends

The end of your auction marks the beginning of the next phase in the sales process, many things will happen and this section covers these.

- How you are likely to be paid – the many different payment options are explained. How you will be informed of payment.

- What to consider when packaging your item to ensure a safe delivery, but also maximise your profit.

- The various issues surrounding dispatch are shown, along with recommendations on best practice.

- How to sell more items to second and third placed bidders; the 'Second Chance' option is explained here.

- This section will also explain how you can claim back eBay fees should your buyer default.

Refine your auction format

Take your eBay auctions to the next level. Create your own look and design your own auction format.

- With fully worked examples, this section shows how to include larger pictures at no extra cost, provide live links to other websites and promote your other auctions. All this is possible with little or no knowledge of computer codes.

- Fully customise your auctions using basic HTML codes which are fully explained. Alter the colour of your auctions and create your own backgrounds and borders. Cross promote your other auctions with live picture links and more. All the codes you need, and an explanation of how to use them, can be found in this section.

Fraud

Learn more about fraud on eBay. Whenever money changes hands, there is the opportunity for fraud and it does happen. This section will highlight the issues around:

- Payment fraud. How to anticipate this situation, what to check for and precautions you should take.

- The possible hijack of your eBay account. You will receive many attempts by third parties who will try to obtain your password and take control of your account. There are many ways to fall foul of these scams and these sections look in more detail at the systems used to guard against these scams and how to spot potential dangers.

- What eBay will and won't do concerning fraud on their site. This section outlines their policy and provides advice on how to proceed if anything does go wrong.

- What to do if you are the victim of fraud. How to put things right with minimum hassle.

Developing your business

Develop your online business and build on your eBay brand. This chapter discusses options to maximise your eBay business for increased sales and higher profits. Included are comprehensive sections on:

- eBay shops. The available options, how much they cost and what advantages you would expect to see. An insight to the various seller tools that are available. How these enhancements can be used to encourage repeat sales from your satisfied customers.

- Finding stock. This is one of the more frustrating aspects of any business. This section describes practical ways to obtain more stock, including the use of eBay as a source of goods for resale.

- How to increase both the exposure of your auctions and your cash flow by becoming an **eBay Affiliate**. What is involved, what the benefits really are and how you can make money simply by passing business to eBay from your own website.

- Power Seller status. What it means and how to make the grade. Is it really good for sales?

- Trading with the global economy. This can appear to be a minefield of red tape and regulations. It is possible to export from the UK with minimum stress, and this section details the requirements and outlines what is really needed.

Manage the paperwork

Keeping on top of the paperwork in any business is a demanding task, and an eBay business is no different. This last section of the book looks at:

- The legal issues surrounding business on the internet and how these impact on requirements such as VAT.

- What your position is regarding tax; both income and capital gains tax will be explained.

- Becoming self-employed. This section delves into more detail about self-employment, how easy it is to register, how exactly you go about it and what it means for things such as National Insurance.

- Your tax return. With any business, comes the need once a year to submit final accounts to the tax office. This section highlights some of the typical costs of an eBay business and provides guidance when calculating your profits from selling on eBay.

At each stage of the book, references are made to my own experiences of selling on eBay, highlighting the pitfalls i've discovered along the way and some of the more interesting ways to make selling both enjoyable and very rewarding.

Introduction

Have you ever wondered what it would be like to be your own boss, to work when you decide to and make as much money as you want? Perhaps you would like to work from home, spend more time with the children and, at the same time, create a business that could grow as large as you wish.

I did, and after just two years selling on eBay I now have all of these things. Following a long career in the world of corporate sales, I became disillusioned and realised that I did indeed yearn for a different way of life.

Two years ago I had no idea what eBay was. But then I was introduced to the site by a friend and was very soon hooked. I realised then that this could be the way to change my life and that of my family.

The last two years has passed so quickly! I have sold in excess of 6,000 items and have a feedback rating in excess of 5,000. I am a Power Seller and list between 3 and 15 items every day for auction. Perhaps the most important aspect of this journey has been that I have achieved this success with my family, working from home. In the early days everybody was involved with packing, sending emails and so on – a real cottage industry.

Now, two years on, I have left full-time work and can concentrate on eBay full time. I work when I want to, and when the sun shines I don't have to work at all. After almost 20 years driving along the motorways of the UK, I can now smile to myself when I hear of traffic jams and congestion as I make another coffee and walk to my office.

My story is not unique by any means; there are thousands of people earning good money from eBay. Some just want to supplement their existing income, some to own their own business and others, such as myself, want a complete change.

I have achieved all this in just two years from a standing start, and I have learnt so much along the way. I send items to every corner of the world and have developed a complete end-to-end process that allows me to sell everything from an unwanted CD to the garden shed. Everything I know about selling on eBay is in this book. If you want to change your lifestyle a little, or maybe make a complete new start, this book will help you get there.

1

A day in the life
of an eBay trader

· ·

A typical day in the life of this eBay trader

· ·

Dear diary................

6.30

My day starts with the rather loud sound of the alarm clock ringing at 6.30. My wife, Debbie, still works part-time, so this wake up call is for her. I snooze through to 7.00. I no longer possess an alarm clock - this was one of the first things to go when I retired from the conventional rat race of life.

7.00

Catch the news headlines on the radio. The weather is set to be good for the next few days, which is welcome as I have some work to do in the garden that I have put off for weeks. (On the other hand, the weather forecast is always wrong and if it rains I can leave the garden again.) Following the weather is the traffic report. This is the most fun to listen to and is certainly worth staying in bed for. Congestion, traffic queues, hold ups on the M25, broken down lorries and lanes coned off - another typical day in the life of a commuter. Back to Zzzland.

7.05

The house starts to stir. With three school-age children (sorry, I mean 'young adults'), the timetable to use the bathroom is extremely tight. In they go, one after the other, while I go downstairs to feed our two dogs. Or rather, the dogs round me up and herd me downstairs towards the food bowls.

7.07

Switch on the kitchen radio and flick on the kettle. This kettle holds a special place in my affections. Since leaving the world of Corporate Sales, the kettle and I have formed a relationship which would be the envy of any courting couple. We spend so much time together and I can turn it on whenever I want. The radio has another news flash: traffic lights not working, ensuing queues, etc. The kettle boils.

7.15

Back upstairs with two cups of tea. Everything is moving along nicely, except the bathroom is still not free -with a houseful of women what do you expect?

7.45

I have managed to grab a bathroom slot and donned my working uniform: shorts, tee-shirt and no socks (don't you just hate wearing socks). No more suits to choose from (sold them on eBay), no more ties to select (sold on eBay), no more shiny black shoes to wear (eBay) and, best of all, no more shirts with collars (even I couldn't sell these on eBay).

Downstairs, the working day is starting. Debbie switches on the main computer and wireless router, which provides broadband connection to the three terminals in the house: one for buying, one for selling, and one for the kids' MSN.

It's time now for the first look at my eBay auctions to see how things are moving.

Lego sales are 'building' well and the Captain Scarlet fancy dress costume has reached £9.55. Having bought 25 of these at £4.60 from a high street shop, it's good to see them so popular. The make-up sets purchased from Boots for £3.32 are selling well at £7.49, and the Wade Whimsies bought for 50p are now at £11.65.

I have 137 auctions live at the moment, with nine ending this evening. The current sales value of these nine is £68.27. eBay auction values tend to rise towards the end of the fixed period duration as the item moves towards the top of the list, so things for today look good so far.

Time to check the emails.

This is always a voyage of discovery as you never really know who has your email address. There are 17 new emails: four of which are offering me over the counter drugs [delete]; a 'great new mortgage deal' [delete]; some 'incredible anti-spyware software' [delete]; and penis enlargement cream [file for future reference].

There are usually three other types of email received:

- spoofs, which will try to solicit passwords and personal details from me,
- questions from potential buyers and, best of all,
- notifications of payments received whilst we have been asleep.

I'll get round to these later, but now it's time for the worker in the household to drop the kids off at school and depart for work.

8.15

The house is quiet at last!

Having spent 24 years working for the same company and many years as a Sales Account Manager pounding the motorways of the UK, my daily commute now consists of an eight yard walk, coffee in hand, to my garden shed - the centre of my eBay operations.

8.20

Time to open up the shed for the day's business.

When I say shed, it is a little bit more than just a shed. This is a purpose built wooden building the size of a single garage, designed for one purpose: to make money. Inside is the third computer terminal. This one is for selling, no games software on this one, no MSN or chat rooms, this is a sleek, mean machine and along with the kettle is the other love of my life (apart from the wife, kids and dogs of course).

The shed, or 'office', also has rack after rack of storage capacity shelving from floor to ceiling, with items to be sorted, items to be listed soon, items currently listed and items sold and not yet shipped. There's storage for packing materials, boxes, bubble wrap, sticky tape and so on. There is an area for photography and another for packing up the sold items. This is my world.

8.30

Let's get started.

Turn the radio on, maybe Classic FM, I'm in a chilled kind of mood today.

The emails need dealing with. The questions from potential buyers are the most important as these guys may move on to another auction if the reply is not quick. There are four at the moment:

- *Do I ship to the USA? [Yes]*
- *Do I combine items to reduce shipping? [Yes]*
- *Will I end the Warhammer auction early for £16? [No]*
- *Do I accept American Dollars cash? [As a last resort]*

The spoof emails are great fun to read, and some of them can be very convincing (I have included a selection at the end of this book). Apparently, in just one night I have been invited to become a Power Seller (again); had my PayPal account accessed by a foreign IP address; face suspension if I don't validate my eBay details immediately; and I need to update my billing details after an eBay audit. Some of the spelling and grammar is just awful.

The rest of the emails are notifications of instant payments into my PayPal account. Although I have been in bed, all over the world other people are awake and as we sell 40% of our items overseas, payments can arrive at any time. Which is just fine by me!

9.00

It's time for the packing to be completed. This is perhaps the most tedious element of my day. It can take anything up to two hours depending on sales. If you can imagine the run up to Christmas and wrapping those presents every day, you will get the idea. Today is not too bad, I should be finished in an hour. The items I sell are all different, the size and weight will vary in almost every case. A seller of DVDs for example, would have an easier time of packing as all of the items are the same shape and weight. For me, the key thing is to anticipate how the item will be packed before it is sold.

I will endeavour to send an item as soon as it has been paid for - this will get them out of the shed and should result in a happy buyer. Today I have predominately toys to send:

- A Disneyland Polly Pocket play-set bought for £2, sold for £23.50 [fairly straightforward, into a box, brown paper, done].

- A fancy dress nurse outfit brought from Toymaster Kingdom for £3, sold for £7.50 [into a bubble bag and away].

- Thomas the Tank Engine train, bought for 20p at a car boot sale, sold for £11 [roll in bubble wrap and into a bubble bag].

This packing lasts for just about an hour. It is not the most interesting of tasks, but the radio was good company and the dogs put in an appearance, sniffed about, stretched a bit and then went back to sleep in the kitchen.

10.00

Step outside into the natural light and look at the garden. It still needs some work. I am just about to roll up my sleeves when thankfully I am distracted by the dogs barking inside. The postman has arrived and a bundle of mail is on the mat. Just time for a quick cup of tea in the garden while I read through it.

It is not a bad day. Two UK cheques have arrived (brilliant, no PayPal fees on these); 45 Euros from a lady in Finland who bought some vintage Lego; and a $14 Postal Money Order from the US (which unfortunately is only negotiable in the US - another email to write later).

There is a great note with one of the cheques from a lady who bought some Winnie The Pooh Duplo for £10.50 for her daughter:

Dear Sir / Madam

Please find enclosed a cheque for £13.50 to pay for the Winnie The Pooh Duplo pieces inc P&P. My little girl will be most appreciative.

This is the first item I have purchased from eBay and I am not sure my nerves can take anymore.

Yours faithfully.

What a great note! I will get this packed up after tea and in the post immediately.

Not waiting for cheques to clear can be asking for trouble, but with a reasonably low value one I am happy to take the chance. In almost three years, only two cheques have bounced.

This note also shows how important first time buyers are. For one thing, they tend to bid more which is good for business. It also shows just how much fun eBay can be. I'll post the toys quickly, send a polite response, leave great feedback for the buyer and they may just visit again.

10.30

Time for a quick check on eBay to see how things are moving.

I have sold another set of comedy DVDs for £4.99 (picked up 36 sets of these for £20); and two rugs in the shape of Bob The Builder at £9 each, which we bought from the discount shop QD for £3.99 each. We bought 48 rugs in total and they are not selling that fast, so may consider reducing the price.

Tonight's items have now reached £76.47. The first item ends at 19.30, so still loads of time for them to go up in value.

I am at a bit of a loose end. Coffee is not until 11.00, I don't really fancy the gardening or any more packing, so it's off to the park with the dogs for a quick walk.

11.00

Coffee time. Our house runs along very traditional lines; coffee at 11.00 and tea at 16.00. Usually I would take some time out to relax a bit with my coffee, but today I have some new stock that I want to get photographed.

Whilst on a day out in Great Yarmouth, we found a shop selling Thomas The Tank Engine model trains for just £1 each. We bought 73. The range has now been discontinued and they should sell for £7 each. I will run each model in a traditional auction to determine the market value and then offer the remaining trains on a 'Buy It Now' basis to move the volume.

Back out in the office, the light is just right for photography. I select the best background colours for the trains and take two pictures of each one, transferring them directly to the computer from time to time.

11.30

The front doorbell rings. There is an extension bell in the shed so that I can hear (the dogs going ballistic also caught my attention). DHL have a huge parcel for us. Debbie has been busy buying again. I suspect that I know what it is, but I am not allowed to open the box. Debbie bought it and has the right to inspect it first - everybody likes to receive a parcel.

I've finished the photography for today. Just time to pack up the Winnie The Pooh Duplo, Lego for Finland, and both Bob The Builder rugs, which have been paid for. Once this is done I have a sack of parcels waiting to be dropped off at the postal depot later this afternoon.

12.00

Time to start preparing for the auctions that will start tonight. I don't use any automated sales tools, but will schedule auctions to start at my preferred times. I also use large pictures within my item descriptions and these will need to be uploaded to my website in advance. As the items to be listed tonight are all very similar (the train photos I took earlier), I only need to write the description once and then use the 'Sell similar' option for the subsequent auctions and slightly alter the pictures.

12.20

Look at the time! I have been so busy that I lost track. Debbie will be home at 12.30 and I promised to do the vacuuming in the house. Rush indoors and quickly push the vacuum around a bit. Just in time. The doorbell rings, the dogs go mad again and Debbie has arrived home.

12.40

It's time for lunch. There's a great sandwich shop in town that does a fantastic brie and bacon panini. It's a nice day, so we decide to leave the car at home and cycle into town. The cycles were one of the first purchases made after I gave up the 9-to-5 work life. We sold the second car and in an attempt to slow down the pace of life, bought two fold up mountain bikes.

Before we go, there is just time to open the large box. As I suspected, it's a huge collection of Brio wooden train track purchased from eBay only three days ago. There is loads here: tunnels, trains, engine sheds, etc. Buying whole collections from eBay and then splitting them into smaller lots can be very lucrative. A large collection cannot be sold overseas as it needs somebody with a large house to store it in and a large bank balance to buy it. In smaller quantities, it can be shipped anywhere, easily packaged and at pocket money prices. We tend to concentrate on toys, but it would work with football programmes, CDs or DVDs and computer games.

14.00

Return home from cycle ride. Dismount gently (this keep-fit stuff does hurt to start with).

A quick check on the auctions' progress shows that the Warhammer Space Marines are now well over the £16 we were offered earlier in the day, and the Fisher Price plastic knights are £10. Whilst out on our bikes, two Buy It Now options were taken for fancy dress costumes, the profit from which will pay for lunch. The total value of tonight's auctions has now topped £90.

Back into the office to finish tonight's auctions. The pictures have been loaded onto the website, and I can begin to write the description of each item and then schedule it to start sometime between 19.30 and 22.00. I manage to get ten items listed in an hour, which is good going. I could do more, but these should bring in £100 plus and I don't want to work all of the time or I might as well get a proper job!

15.00

Time to pick up the kids from school and walk the dogs again. On the way I drive past my local postal depot and drop off my sack of parcels

15.30

Return home with two very tired dogs, they are still not used to the extra walking, and three young adults with attitude.

16.00

Tea time.

A nice cup of tea and time to catch up with the day's events. It's good to put your feet up now and then - I still don't fancy the gardening. The local paper has arrived and Debbie (Chief Buyer) is scanning the small ads for anything that might just make a profit. Nothing today it seems.

It's time to check the email again.

There is another offer of a cheap mortgage and a replica Rolex watch, just for me. I don't even own a watch anymore. Two more questions from interested bidders:

- Do we ship to the USA? [Yes]. There is a pattern forming here. No matter how big you write 'WE SHIP ANYWHERE', you will still get the same question.

- The second email is asking if we have a fancy dress costume in another size. [Unfortunately, no.]

There is not much to do for the rest of the day. The auctions start to end at 19.30 and I will watch them end if we are about. Even after many thousands of sales, it is still a fantastic feeling to see the last minute increase in value as the final seconds tick away.

Debbie has placed a number of items into our buying 'watch list', so we run through these and check the potential for profits. Some sellers are just so bad at selling their items, that another seller can buy them, present them in a better way and make money. This is our aim here. Today we see a collection of eight Lilliput Lane cottages with a current auction price of £8. They weigh so much that they cannot be sold outside of the UK and the description is very poor. Referring to our buyer guide, we think these models could be worth between £40 and £60, so they are certainly worth keeping an eye on.

Also on the watch list is a large Playmobil mansion house, shown in a box - not its original box - just a load of bits in a brown box. Pictures sell items. This seller did not assemble the house, so we have to rely on the description to work out the value. It includes quite a lot of furniture, which is always popular. The current price is £30, another one to watch.

17.30

Preparation for the evening meal, not by me though. There is an understanding in the house that Debbie prepares the meals and I will recycle the dishes and tidy up afterwards. I'm just leaving a few feedback comments for recent buyers. I tend to do these in batches as it can turn into a chore if you leave it too long.

Just time to check on the day's business. Not a lot of change. Tonight's auctions now total £92.35, but as they all end in the time period after dinner and before bedtime I am confident they will rise further.

Tonight I am selling mainly toys, so have timed the auctions to end after the evening meal is finished and before children go to bed. This should ensure that the young ones are still around to coax mum into one final bid to secure the toy they have set their heart on. I know it sounds mean, but it's a dog eat cyber-dog world and think how the child would feel if mum lost out for a pound.

19.00

Dinner is over, and the children have even done some of the washing up. The dogs have been fed and the house starts to wind down from the hectic day. The kids drift away to their rooms to watch the music channel instead of doing homework and I can settle back ready to watch the auctions end.

A quick check of the emails reveals the usual last minute questions from bidders who have just spotted our auctions:

- Do you combine lots and reduce shipping? [Yes, no problem.]
- Do you accept PayPal from the USA? [We accept PayPal from anywhere.]
- Do you ship to the USA? [**!!*!! Yes, we would love to - Note to self, must write in a bigger font size]

19.25

Tonight's auctions are about to end.

This is the exciting bit, what it has all been for.

The total sales value for the nine items is now £103.35, none of the items have increased significantly, just the odd bid here and there.

First up is half a kilo of assorted Lego pieces. These are left over when I sort out all the premium pieces such as windows and figures. The current price is £8.60 going into the final moments. I like to make £10 a kilo, so this is about right. No movement in the final seconds and the auction closes at £8.60.

There is a ten minute gap between my auction end times. I am keen that should a bidder be interested in more than one item, they are not rushed. I leave just enough time for them to recover from one auction and prepare for last minute bidding on the next. Always let your customers buy in a relaxed way.

19.35

My next auction ends in 5 minutes. It's a Star Wars Lego set, quite nice, no box, but most of the pieces are here and four great pictures really showed it to it's best. It's had 18 bids so far and the price is currently £22. This is a reasonable price - it took me an hour to build a few days back. Two bidders are showing an interest, one in the UK and the other in France. The price moves up another £2 and the set is destined for a trip across the channel. The UK bidder acts again, but still is not a high bidder, the price is £26. Into the final few seconds and they think it's all over...it is now, a new bidder from Italy with 250 feedbacks to their name has come over the top of the French bidder and taken the set for £32. They must have put in a large proxy bid, but we will never know just how much they were prepared to pay.

19.40

Not a bad start to the evening, time to make a coffee.

19.45

As the next auction is almost about to end an email arrives, someone has bought two fancy dress witch costumes with a 'Buy It Now' option for £13 and paid as well.

The next auction is for a Fisher Price model helicopter and trucks from the old (I mean vintage) airport set. The auction high bidder really wants this model. They are in Canada, with only one feedback score and have placed three proxy bids. (Proxy bidding is the eBay system that allows you to place your maximum bid now - the system then bids on your behalf up to your maximum.) They are currently winning at £8.50. Placing multiple proxy bids shows that a buyer is determined to win, although with a more unscrupulous seller, this technique can cost the bidder dearly.

No movement. Still, it's a fair price. No movement that is, until, with 20 seconds to go, a bidder with 1,639 feedbacks in the UK enters a bid that removes all three proxy bids and takes the helicopter for £16. The winner turns out to be a collector of Fisher Price models, we get on great and another eBay friendship is formed.

I hate to think of that poor child in Canada who has an airport, but no helicopter - every child should have a helicopter. As I have another set with the same models, I make an immediate second chance offer to them. Moments later they have accepted for a price of £15.

I love it when the second chance offer is taken. They do have to be made as soon as possible, while the bidder is reeling from the defeat and getting an ear bashing from their children. I will make identical lots whenever I can just in anticipation of this.

19.50

Another ten minute gap. Time for a quick email check - nothing of interest here. The first auctions scheduled to start tonight have begun their ten day duration. These auctions will have a 15 minute interval, which will make things less rushed in ten days time.

My next auction is for a Playmobil construction site digger. It's a nice toy, quite large and still available with a retail price of about £15. The price is £7.09, the current high bidder is in the UK with a feedback score of 66. The seconds tick away and no more bids are forthcoming, so it sells for £7.09. Not bad, as I picked it up at a car boot sale for 50p.

With the running total for the evening at £78.69, and still five auctions to end, I am quite pleased.

20.00

The first payments are starting to arrive for tonight's sales; I will need to send some invoices, but will do that later.

The fifth auction to end is for 6cm of used Pokemon trading

cards. I have no idea which of these cards is of value to a collector, so I sell them by the cm - 6cm should be worth between £7 and £10. This auction has had 276 hits, so they are still very popular. The current price is £7.57, which is where it ends. A little on the low side. I do have some more, but the second bid is £7.07, right on the lower threshold of my price range, so I won't make a second chance this time.

20.05

Next up is a selection of Fisher Price plastic knights from a huge castle set. I buy the castle with the knights and then dispose of the castle: the packing would be horrendous, whereas the knights can fit into a small box. I paid £4 for the castle and 15 knights. I have been watching these throughout the day and the current price is £14. At £1 per figure, it's about what I would expect.

20.06

The bid on the knights has risen to £22 - this is very good, that's tomorrow's lunch paid for. Now it's £24.40, the second bidder with two feedbacks is now winning again, let's hope they both really need some more knights for their castle.

20.07

Up to £26.40. Still with the newer bidder. Then £30, I think I will have some wine with my lunch.

20.08

The current high bidder is still the fairly new eBay member with 2 feedbacks and at such a high price I now begin to wonder if payment will be OK. Fingers crossed that this is not the end.

20.09

With about one minute to go, the bid rises to £32, and the winning bidder changes again. 28 seconds later the bid is up another £2 and the new member is again winning. A further 10 seconds later it is £35, still with the same bidder.

20.10

It's all over. The final bid was for £37, the winner was the bidder with two feedbacks from Banbury, Oxfordshire and they paid straight away with PayPal. The second bidder had also bid £37, but as it was registered later they did not win.

That was great for me, I enjoyed it. Time for a cigarette (as I don't smoke it will have to be a virtual one). That was the last of the toys for tonight. There are still three Warhammer auctions to end, but they finish later in the evening as I am trying to capture the American buyers. I'll come back later to see how they do.

The current tally is £123.26. I am pleased with this. Time to check on the other members of the household: both dogs fast asleep; all children safely tucked up with soaps or Sky telly; and Debbie chilled out with a good book.

It's around 20.30, time to unwind in front of the TV for a while. It was not so long ago that I would have been returning from a business trip to Leeds or wherever at about this time; hot, flustered and with loads of emails to catch up with. Oh, how I miss it!

23.00

That's it for another day. The Warhammer auctions went OK. Time to lock up the house and off to bed. It's been a funny old day, I didn't seem to get a minutes rest. Might have to take the day off tomorrow. And I never did get the gardening done - oh well, there's always next week.

Starting out

Overview

They do say that the longest journey starts with the first step, which in the case of an eBay business is certainly true. The great thing about starting an online business and selling on eBay is that you control how long the journey will be and how fast you want to travel.

With just one item to sell and around 15 pence to invest, you will be in business.

How big your business grows will depend on many things, which may also vary over the fullness of time. The beginning, however, will be a similar experience for the largest corporate undertaking or the smallest sole trader with only the germ of an idea of what they want to do.

This first chapter introduces you to eBay, how it was formed and how big it really is, who sells on eBay, what is permitted and just why eBay is the ideal medium to fulfil your ambitions.

Without a plan, all you have is a set of good intentions, so this section will show you the process to create a plan that suits you. It will be nothing to do with a computer or using the internet, but instead a close up look at the aspects you would like to see from your new undertaking. Included are some thoughts about:

- how to get design ideas;
- what you could sell;
- who you could sell to; and
- how you would like to be paid.

What exactly is eBay?

eBay is an online marketplace that enables trade on a national and international basis. It consists of millions of people that together form a trading community consisting of individuals and businesses all using the eBay systems to trade millions of items every day.

When the internet came along, it offered the ability to improve many services. For example, *Amazon* became famous by creating a great online bookshop. But, in essence, *Amazon* was still just like a mail-order bookshop – just faster and cheaper. However, online auctions, led by eBay, were revolutionary. Without the internet, they could not exist. It is the internet that gives them their power by allowing an audience of millions to share the service.

To say that eBay is big hardly does it justice. eBay is huge, and it is still growing. There are now more than 125 million registered users of eBay. At the time of writing, eBay operates in 31 countries and allows any member in any country to trade with any other member.

eBay is the platform for trade that can be used by businesses and individuals alike. It has removed an entire level of the supply chain and put manufacturers and wholesalers directly in contact with the end consumer.

Items sold on eBay are classified in a system of categories and sub-categories. There are thousands of these categories which ensures that any item has a logical location within the site. On any given day there are millions of items for sale, including antiques, toys, books, computers, sporting goods, photography and cars. The items listed on eBay fall into two main types:

1.   Those you can bid on, just as you would do in any traditional auction,

and

2.   those items that have a fixed price, where you have the option to purchase them immediately ('Buy It Now'), just as you would do in any retail outlet or shop.

eBay background

Founded in the USA in 1995, eBay.com was originally intended as a trading site for collectors of various items such as *Pez* sweet dispensers and *Beanie Babies*. eBay has now become much more, and almost anything is available through the site.

eBay in figures

Some current facts and figures that help give an idea of the world of eBay.

---

eBay figures

- eBay.co.uk is the UK's **largest online marketplace**.
- eBay.co.uk hit the **10 million users** milestone in February 2005.
- There are more than **3 million items** for sale on the site at any one time on eBay.co.uk.
- eBay.co.uk has over **13,000 categories**.
- At any given time, there are approximately **78 million listings** worldwide.
- The **most expensive item** sold on eBay to date is a private business jet for $4.9 million.
- eBay has **181 million registered** users worldwide.
- More than **724,000 professional sellers in the** US use eBay as a primary or secondary source of income.
- In 2004, gross merchandise volume (GMV), the value of all successfully closed listings on eBay.co.uk reached a **record $3.7 billion**.
- There were **546.4 million new listings** added to eBay worldwide in the fourth quarter of 2005.
- At the end of the fourth quarter 2005, eBay hosted approximately **383,000 stores worldwide**, with approximately **212,000 stores hosted on the US site** and **171,000 stores** hosted on eBay's international sites.

---

eBay.co.uk

Founded in October 1999, eBay.co.uk is now the UK's largest online marketplace and the number one e-commerce site. In December 2004, over a third of all active internet users visited eBay.co.uk.

On eBay UK:

- There are over three million items for sale at any one time.

- The number of registered users reached 10m in February 2005.

An average day

On an average day on eBay UK, someone buys a:

- mobile phone every 21 seconds;

- laptop every 2 minutes;

- MP3 player every 2 minutes;

- car every 2 minutes; and a

- woman's handbag every 36 seconds.

What sells on eBay

There is no doubt that eBay is big and getting bigger every year as more and more individuals and businesses discover the benefits that this marketplace has to offer.

But what actually sells on the site and how do you make money from it?

Almost anything can be sold through eBay – even the kitchen sink (which I sold for my brother-in-law for £150). There are some prohibited items (more on these below) and some items are not worth anything. Apart from that, almost everything that has a value can be put up for auction – and it seems that even things that don't appear to have any value can also find buyers. With prices for items starting at just one penny and with a ten million pound upper limit, everything will find it's own level.

TIP Choose a product you already know something about and enjoy working with. Consider issues such as: how you will acquire your stock, where you will store it, and what will be involved with shipping.

As an example, during June 2005 the following items sold on eBay:

- 54 Rubik cubes with an average sale price of £3.75.

- 18 copies of the Wombles on DVD with an average sale price of £3.95.

- 368 BMW keyrings with an average sales price of £2.67.

- 27 collapsible heated swimming pools with an average sales price of £220,

- 36 domestic stairlifts with an average sales price of £2,250.

Over the past two years I have sold thousands of different items, including two garden sheds, a washing machine, a full size Queen Mother armorial flag, a Spike Milligan concert advertising poster, our family car as well as almost everything in the house that is not nailed down.

I am always trying different things and will, as the saying goes, try anything once, although I have not yet tried to sell autumn leaves, a snowman, genuine mud from a very wet rock festival, a jar of pickle or an empty box, but all of these items have been put up for auction – and sold!

Prohibited items

Is my item allowed on eBay?

eBay have set out guidelines to help sellers decide if their items should be sold on the site. The list below is not exhaustive (there are more details available through the eBay online help sections), but this list provides a very clear indication of what cannot be sold. Everything not listed below would probably be OK to sell. eBay has three definitions of items that may not be allowed to be sold.

> Selling alcohol on eBay is generally not allowed; although if the container is deemed to be collectable, it is possible to sell the bottle or tin with the contents intact. Selling a selection of bottled beers from the early to mid eighties, I received an email asking if the beer itself would be OK to drink. I replied that there was a likelihood that the beer would be off by now. They didn't bid on them.

1.   *Prohibited*: means that these items must not be listed on eBay.

2.   *Questionable*: means that items may be listed under certain conditions.

3.   *Potentially Infringing*: means that items may be in violation of certain copyrights, trademarks or other rights.

A list of prohibited items can be found in the appendices.

What will eBay do with these listings?

eBay has a strong sense of community and to a degree is self-policing. Other members will report items that contravene the rules. To quote eBay on this:

> *"eBay reserves the right to delete any listing that may violate any legal provision or the general principles and values of the community at large, even if the legal provision or principles and values are not explicitly stated on the eBay site."*

This basically means that in some cases, eBay will make a judgement as they best see it.

Who sells on eBay

The eBay community is made up of buyers and sellers who visit the site to trade. This might include large companies, small companies, individuals running a business from home, or individuals just trying to clear out an attic.

Anybody who is over 18 can register, and within a short while can buy or sell. To many, eBay has become more than just a trading site; a sense of real community exists with those individuals who have been using the site for a while. Discussion boards are very popular, not only for exchanging experiences, but also for meeting new virtual friends.

eBay has over 100 million members worldwide, selling 25 million items at any one time. eBay.co.uk is part of the eBay network. All of these 100 million members will have access to your auctions and could become your customers. These eBay members could also be your competitors as they can market to the UK in the same way that we can direct our sales to another country.

The eBay community

eBay is a collective of many individuals, each with a common goal: to either buy or sell in a pleasant rewarding environment. Information and knowledge is freely exchanged between members via a number of user forums or discussion boards. The discussion forums are found under the 'Community' tab on the eBay website.

Almost any question can be posted on to the system, and anybody browsing through the forums can choose to reply – both question and answer are available for all to see and learn from. There are discussion boards for a whole range of issues: one specifically for new users, one about postage and payments and even a discussion board for HTML concerns.

TIP When starting out on your selling career with eBay, refer back to these boards from time to time, as, if you have a problem, it is certain that someone else will have a similar concern and you may just find the answer.

eBay Power Sellers have a dedicated discussion board where more complex issues can be discussed. Many Power Sellers also patrol the general forums offering their experience to those who ask.

Through the discussion boards, members meet and get to know each other, discuss topics of mutual interest and help each other to learn all about eBay.

eBay can become part of a member's lifestyle. Many members have created second businesses, or left day jobs altogether, by trading on eBay. For hundreds of thousands of others, eBay is the place to share a passion for items that are collectable or special in some way.

As mentioned the community is self-policing, and users frequently form 'neighbourhood watch' groups to help guard against misuse or violations of site etiquette.

eBay encourages open and honest communication between the community and the company. Members of the community often give their feedback to improve the environment in which they spend their time.

The fundamental principle that eBay employs is that every trader, whether large or small, has the same set of rules for trading – larger companies do not receive a discount on fees or any form of preferential treatment, it is a level playing field.

The eBay values

eBay was founded on five key values and the eBay.co.uk site also holds these at its heart. As with all systems and markets, there will be those who break the rules and go against the interests of the community, however these amount to only a very small proportion of eBay users. With a little caution and some help from the recommendations within this book, you will be able to avoid most pitfalls and trade successfully in an environment where a problem is very much the exception.

The five key eBay values

1. eBay believe that people are basically good.

2. eBay recognises and respects everyone as a unique individual.

3. eBay believes everyone has something to contribute.

4. eBay encourages people to treat others the way that they want to be treated.

5. eBay believes that an honest, open environment can bring out the best in people.

Reading these values for the first time can seem a little strange (and might seem rather too American for British tastes!), but after you have been involved with the site for some time you will find that the community at large generally upholds these values.

First steps

The actual process of selling on eBay is quite straightforward. There are help pages on the website and the sales process will guide you through each stage. You may already have bought on the site and have an understanding of the layout and be familiar with some of the eBay jargon. If not, there is a glossary of terms and abbreviations at the back of this book which should provide some assistance.

This section is about some of the things you will need to know before you start to sell on eBay.

First, it is important to understand some of the background. I will talk about the equipment you will need, who supplies it and, most importantly, how much it is likely to cost.

> When I started, I charged straight into selling. I had not bought anything before and did not understand anything. I have now learnt and adapted over time, but can't help thinking how many mistakes I could have avoided with a little more preparation in the early days.

Understanding the implications, both on your time and your finances, will prepare you for the following section which will look at the subject of what to sell. *It's all about planning.*

TIP Consider buying a few low price items to get started. Not only will this boost your feedback score, but it will also give you an insight into the buyer's point of view, which you can use when selling your own items.

The equipment you need

To place an item for auction on eBay could cost you as little as 15p, but this of course does not take into account the other equipment that is required. The size of your business will determine the cost of starting out, but a very basic eBay trader will need the following.

1. Computer

An up to date computer. These start from about £400 (or cheaper on eBay!) for a desktop model and a little more for a laptop. Older computers will work, but may have some restrictions. It may be worth considering the purchase of a second-hand computer if funds are tight.

> I currently have three computers networked together, one Packard Bell, one Hewlett Packard and one from Time Computers. They all work well together and the support from these companies has been good.

Reference

*   Hewlett Packard (www.hp.co.uk)

*   Packard Bell (www.packardbell.co.uk)

*   Dell (www.dell.co.uk)

2. Digital camera

A good quality picture will enhance your auction more than anything else. A mid-range camera will start from around £70.

To give an idea of cost, but not necessarily a recommendation, the following prices were taken from the internet during June 2005:

*   Canon Powershot S1 IS – £250 from Comet (www.comet.co.uk) Features: 3.3 Mega-pixel, 10x Optical Zoom, Standard Point and Shoot, Video Capability

*   Casio Exilim Zoom Ex-Z55 – £185 from Pixmania (www.pixmania.com) Features: 5.25 Megapixel, 3x Optical Zoom, Compact, Video Capability

*   Fuji Finepix F810 – £236 from ebuyer (www.ebuyer.com) Features: 6.63 Megapixel, 4x Optical Zoom, Standard Point and Shoot, Video Capability

3. Internet connection

Broadband is not required, but it is now so cheap (at around £18 per month) that not having it can be a false economy – the extra speed is well worth the investment. Dial up connections will cost around £10 per month depending upon your package.

Check to see if your home or office can accept broadband at www.broadbandchecker.co.uk

Broadband is offered by a number of suppliers and can be delivered via ADSL, cable or satellite links.

TIP Check with your broadband supplier about download limits. BT, for example, have a monthly limit with their basic package, and, if exceeded, the service will cost you around 20% more that month.

The major broadband suppliers are:

- BT Broadband (www.bt.com/broadband)

- Tiscali (www.tiscali.co.uk)

- AOL (www.aol.co.uk)

- Virgin (www.virgin.net)

- Wanadoo (www.wanadoo.co.uk)

- Onetel (www.onetel.co.uk)

Broadband can be supplied via your cable operator if they operate in your area. The two main companies are:

- NTL (www.home.ntl.com)

- Telewest (www.telewest.co.uk)

Satellite broadband can be delivered by:

- AVC (www.avcbroadband.com)

4. Security software

Anti-virus, firewall and other security software are required to stop rogue programs attacking your computer. Some of these programs can be downloaded directly from the internet with no charge.

The threat posed by the internet to unprotected computers can be very real. This is a topic that deserves more focus, and the next section will deal with the different types of threat and give some suggestions as to protection that can be used.

Tips for safe computing

With all the bad press concerning viruses and computers crashing, it can seem inevitable that your computer will be affected in some way. You can minimise these risks by taking certain precautions; below I have listed a few that will help. Practice 'safe computing' and you should remain free from infection.

- Be suspicious of **attachments** that arrive on emails from unknown sources.

- Some viruses can send emails and attachments that appear to have been **sent by people you know**. If in any doubt, confirm with the sender that they did in fact send it.

- Do not set your email program to **'auto-run' attachments**.

- Keep your computer **fully updated** with all security releases.

- **Back up** all of your important data regularly and keep the back up copies in a safe location.

What can be done to cure an infection

No matter how safe you make your computer and how vigilant you are, there is the chance that your system will become infected. If you suspect that something is wrong, run all of the anti-virus programs that you have installed. This may remove the

> I use a software program called Pest Patrol. It costs about £20 and works with my anti-virus software and firewall. You can check them out at: www.pestpatrol.com

problem. Some infections are easy to remove, others require more serious action. There are a range of programs commercially available on the internet which tackle specific types of problem.

TIP Take your computer for a complete service once a year. This will remove any infections and speed up it's operation. You MOT the car, so do the same with your computer. A full service will cost about £100.

How much time does eBay take?

One of the most attractive aspects of running a business on eBay is the choice you have to work as little or as much as you like. There are, of course, some restrictions. There are only so many hours in the day and the stock you sell may run out, but, as a general rule, the more time you spend selling on eBay, the more money you will make.

The number of auctions that you have on eBay will depend on your own circumstances. However, the greater the volume, the more work it will take to manage them. As a guide, I find my time spent on different activities divides roughly as follows:

- Packing – 30%

- Posting – 20%

- Research – 10%

- After sales paperwork – 10%

- Admin – 10%

- Sourcing products – 20%

I tend to place new auctions every day – the daily quantity will vary between three per day up to fifteen per day during the Christmas season. Due to the nature of the tasks involved in an online business, it is possible to complete them over a period of time rather than all at once. This is something I have found to be a great advantage, as I can break up my day and pursue my other interests.

What to sell

Knowing what to sell and what to avoid are key elements of a successful online business and, in this section, I will share my experiences and provide recommendations to get your business off to a flying start.

Deciding what to sell on eBay may be immediately obvious for you. For example, you may already have a hobby that could produce an income. You may already have access to a stock of items and need a way to sell them. But if you do not yet know what to sell, this section should provide a few ideas.

It is certainly worth checking the wider eBay site to understand what sells in your area of interest. This will not only provide you with an insight into the viability of your particular product, but also show you the techniques used by other eBay sellers.

Start with an easy item

Understanding the sales process is as important as having the right items to sell. Start by selling something that is easy to describe and post – it does not have to be of high value. This will allow you to gain experience of the eBay systems and highlight some improvements that you could make second time around. Once you have mastered the process of selling on eBay, almost anything can be sold in much the same way.

 TIP Consider consumer goods such as CDs, DVDs, clothes or household electronics. These should carry relatively high margins, depending upon your wholesaler.

An easy way to start selling, and to start building up a good feedback score, is to sell unwanted household items. Don't throw away your old camera, somebody will buy it for spares, also hang on to your empty ink jet cartridges, they fetch about £5 a pair. Even the small complementary bars of soap that you pick up in hotel rooms have a value on eBay!

The great thing about selling your own surplus items is that, while it is the selling knowledge that is important, any money made from the sale is a bonus. You will begin to understand how the sales process works, and also get an idea of how much time it all takes.

The more sales you make, the higher your feedback score will become, which will begin to build your eBay reputation.

Establishing yourself as a trustworthy trader is a key element of a successful eBay business. Your potential bidders have little else to go on except your past trading history, recorded within your feedback score. Not only is the numerical value important, but also the comments made by those you have traded with.

If you are just starting out with little feedback, bidders may avoid high value items you are selling as you have no track record. Once you are established, with good feedback, bidders will be prepared to pay more for your items.

Not only will selling your unwanted items boost your feedback, you will also create some capital along the way which can be used to buy stock.

What to avoid

We have already looked at the items that are not allowed on eBay, but there are also some other products that have their own issues that are worth bearing in mind before deciding to sell them.

- Fragile items
  Glass, china and collectables can be fragile and the condition is everything to the avid collector. Consider the implications of more secure packaging both on cost and time.

- Heavy items
  Posting heavy items will cost more money. Sending heavy items overseas, particularly those with low sales value, may incur higher money transaction fees. These will eat into your profit as the fees are calculated on the total amount of money transferred, including the postage charges.

- **Country specific**

  Selling items that are targeted at only one country will restrict your market. Some items only work in restricted regions, such as DVDs and videos.

- **Large items**

  Large items may only be suitable for collection, or may require specialist transportation which will cost more to arrange. Consider the implications of any additional packing requirements – will you need non-standard boxes? Can you deliver large items and, if so, within what geographic area? Collection from your home or place of work may be inconvenient and this may also restrict your market.

- **High value items**

  The higher the value of your items, the more interest there will be from fraudsters who exploit the system. You are unlikely to be defrauded for a second-hand CD, but a valuable watch might be a target. (There are precautions that can be taken to guard against fraud on eBay, and these are covered in a later section.)

Unbundling collections

If you are going to sell a collection of items, consider selling them in several smaller lots. This may attract more bidders who may not want to buy a whole collection. If you have enough of the item to sell a second batch, make the two lots exactly the same as this will give the option for a 'second chance offer', which will be explained a little later and will also save taking more pictures for the next auction.

Selling your items one at a time, rather than in a larger lot may have more appeal to certain collectors. When selling a series of books for example, a collector may be prepared to bid on one, but be put off if the auction includes several that they do not need.

> When selling an old washing machine with a value of £50 or so, I received a bid from Bradford, some 200 miles away. I had stipulated that the item was for collection only and emailed the bidder to confirm. They seemed happy to make such a long journey and, although they were later out-bid, it did show how far some people would travel to collect.

When to sell

There are no fixed rules as to the timing of your auctions, when you sell will probably depend upon your other commitments. If you sell frequently, your cash flow will improve as you will turn your stock round more frequently. If you sell less often but list more items, then you must expect a very busy time when the auctions end.

Seasonal trading

Just as retail outlets on the high street will change their range according to the season, you may also decide to do the same. Toys and gifts will sell better at Christmas, and clothes should be sold according to the season. Collectables and regularly used items such as batteries, seem to have a steady market all year round.

> During the summer months I alter my sales strategy, selling more collectables and large bulky items. I save my main stock of toys for the Christmas rush, which starts in September.

Sales tend to trail off during the hot summer months as people spend less time in front of their computers and more time in the garden. During this period it would be advisable to list items for the minimum price you need for the item as you may get fewer bids to push prices higher.

TIP As a general rule, sell things during the summer months that are likely to be used by the bidder themselves. Items such as replacement parts, collectables, spares for domestic appliances, and so on. During the run up to Christmas, sell things that make ideal gifts that the bidder may well buy for someone else.

Christmas trading

The Christmas trading period deserves a special mention as it is something you have to see to believe. I have now completed two Christmas selling periods and this year I started preparing in June. To say things get hectic is an understatement. To say that anything you put up for sale will sell and make crazy money...is probably right!

After the summer slump when bidders are on the beach or outside with the BBQ, comes the realisation that Christmas is only a few weeks away. When the children go back to school in September, something happens to the nation's buyers; they all seem to enter a buying frenzy.

If you are selling overseas and sending items by surface post, then the last day for sending them is somewhere around mid-October, so you will get overseas interest in September as well.

How to cope with the rush

There are a few things you can do in the anticipation of high sales during this period:

- Prepare your inventory of items, stock up well and tailor your items towards Christmas presents. Put away the Dyson spares and find the Lego.

- Take as many pictures as you can during the summer when times are quieter and the natural light is better. Store these away on your computer.

- Stock up on packaging materials well in advance. My output trebles at this time of year, so having enough boxes and bubble wrap is essential.

- Anticipate the time it will take to complete the packing and listing. Don't undertake major home improvements over this period and you may need to take time off work if things get really manic.

- Recruit additional help – rope the family into some packing duties.

TIP Work hard In the run up to Christmas, don't sleep at all, then take the next three months off.

Frequency of trading

Your other commitments may mean that you can only list items once a week, or even once a month, or you may choose to list items every day. Each has their own advantages and disadvantages. Trial and error will help you find the best policy for your particular item.

TIP Listing several similar auctions at the same time may impact on your final price as the supply increases. Consider running auctions over a fewer number of days to maintain demand.

I made the decision to list items every day. I even list on Christmas day and these auctions will get hits and bids. My main reason to list frequently is twofold: firstly to maintain a shop window, where regular customers will check back to see what new items we have for sale. The second major reason is that every night I will have items in the 'Going, Going, Gone' section, which I feel improves my last minute impulse bids.

Research the market

Having given some thought as to the items you would like to sell, it is now time to see who else is in this marketplace.

This section will demonstrate how to find items and users on eBay and give a few ideas of things to look for when viewing other auctions.

eBay has its own search engines that appear all over the site. These can be used to find both items and other users. As with all internet search engines, you type in your search requirements and the results are displayed. On eBay there are basic and advanced search facilities available I will explain both procedures below.

How eBay users find items

Items can be found on eBay by using two different methods: you can search for them, either by name or by an item number, or you can browse through the site and see what turns up.

Factette: 75% of items are found via the search facility, only 25% are found by browsing.

Using the browse facility

When an item is placed onto the system, each seller must select a category from a list in which to place their item. There are hundreds of different categories available to choose from. [I will go into more detail about selecting the best category when I talk about placing the first auction a little later.]

The browse facility starts by accessing the site map from the menu at the very top of an eBay page. The site map has several areas of interest, but to find an item, we need to browse the categories. The categories are continually changing: as items become popular, a category is added and as interest fades, categories are removed.

Currently the main categories on the site are:

Antiques & Art	Jewellery & Watches
Automotive	Mobile & Home Phones
Baby	Music
Books, Comics & Magazines	Musical Instruments
Business, Office & Industrial	PC & Video Gaming
Clothes, Shoes & Accessories	Photography
Coins	Pottery, Porcelain & Glass
Collectables	Sporting Goods
Computing	Sports Memorabilia
Consumer Electronics	Stamps
Crafts	Tickets & Travel
Dolls & Bears	Toys & Games
DVD, Film and TV	Wholesale & Job Lots
Health & Beauty	Everything Else
Home & Garden	

When you click on a main category, a number of subcategories will be shown. You can browse through the entire subcategory or select an area of specific interest. Narrowing your selection of category will result in fewer items to browse through. If you were interested in some speakers for your Hi-Fi system, your category selection would be:

Consumer Electronics
   Home Audio / HI-FI
     Speakers
       Floor Standing

The list displayed will be all the items placed into this category by the sellers. It will not include any speakers incorrectly listed and may well include items that don't belong in this category. (See Fig 1. opposite.)

Fig 1. Browse screen

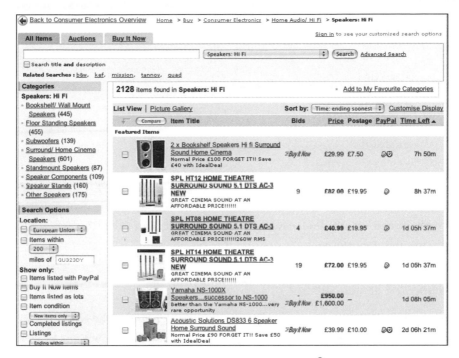

Results display

The results can be displayed in a number of ways. The default standard is to show them by time with the auctions ending soonest at the top of the list. You can alter this display by selecting an alternative from the 'Sort by' menu. The current options are:

- **Time**
  Ending soonest
  Newly listed
  Ending today
  New today

- **Price**
  Highest first
  Lowest first

- **Distance**
  Nearest first

- **Condition**
  New first
  Used first

- **Payment**
  PayPal first
  PayPal last

As you will have seen by using the Browse facility, selecting the incorrect category can have a significant impact on the price that an item reaches. [When I look at the first auction in more detail in a later chapter, I will discuss this area further.]

Using the search facility

Finding the item you want quickly is a fundamental part of the eBay system. In much the same way that some shoppers will visit a large town and browse through shops all day, others will want to get the shopping over with as soon as possible.

We have looked at the browse function, now it is time to understand more about how the other 75% of eBay users find things: they search for them.

The search facility within eBay is very efficient, it can be used for simple searches or for quite complex and detailed searches. This section shows how the search facilities work, including some of the more unusual options.

Simple search

Simple search engines are on almost every page within eBay and they look like this:

Fig 2. Simple search engine

To use the search facility, type in the name of the item you are looking for and click the search button. Typing in a general word such as 'bucket' will return hundreds of results – 1,058, when I tried it. Finding the particular type of bucket you want from this size of list would be very difficult. Changing the search to 'plastic bucket' would return a smaller list: in this case, only 13 items to look through.

The more specific the search, the fewer results are displayed and the easier it is to find an item.

Another example. This time I'm searching for 'golf clubs'. I see there are 732 auctions active with the words 'golf clubs' in the title. I can narrow this search further as the results are shown by the category that they are placed in. I am actually after a vintage golf club and there are only 19 auctions in the 'Golf Memorabilia' category.

As you can see, this search function is very basic. It will just return any auctions which contain the search words in the title.

NOTE

eBay searches are not case-sensitive, so whether you use capital letters or not, your results will be the same.

Advanced search

Links to the advanced search engine appear next to the simple search box – just click on the link and a whole new set of search options will be available.

These advanced search options can be combined to allow for a more focused search, or they can be used one at a time. I have listed what I consider to be the most useful advanced search options below:

Fig 3. Advanced search engine

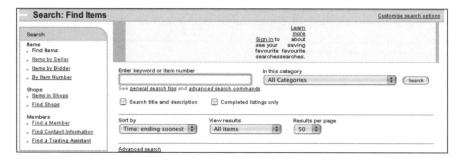

- **Search title and description**

  As the name suggests, if you tick this box, eBay will search for your keywords both in the title and in the description of the item. With this option selected, the same search for my 'plastic bucket' now returns 247 results.

> **TIP** When selling items, ensure that your description contains all the keywords that describe your item. Even if you cannot fit them into the title, put them in the description.

- **Buy It Now items**

  By ticking this box, your results will show the auctions with your search words in the title that have the option for an instant purchase. There was only one plastic bucket, a 'Yellow Fire & Ice Plastic Ice Bucket' for only £3. I was tempted!

By combining the 'Buy It Now' option with the Title and Description search, 65 auctions were displayed.

The results shown from this last search were quite diverse as any auction with the words 'plastic' and 'bucket' somewhere in the description would have been shown. This can be overcome by telling eBay to search for your keywords in a specific way. These techniques can save a lot of time when searching:

- Two or more words somewhere in the title in no particular order. Just enter the words separated with a space. This is how the examples above worked.

- The words you are looking for need to be in a particular order, i.e. War of the Worlds.

  Type in the words and put quotation marks around them, i.e. "War of the Worlds". Only items with this exact phrase will be shown.

- You could be looking for items that don't contain a certain word. For example, if searching for hiking boots, but not brown ones. Type in the search words 'hiking boots' and then the word 'brown' with a minus sign immediately in front of it, i.e. "Hiking Boots –brown". This will show all auctions with 'hiking boots' in the title, except those that also have the word 'brown'.

- You may be looking for items that do not contain several words, maybe pottery items, but not Denby, Poole or Wedgwood. Place the words you do not want inside brackets and separate them with commas. The search would look like this: "Pottery – (Denby, Poole, Wedgwood)".

- If you are looking for any item relating to a particular theme, you can just type in the first few letters and eBay will search for any words that begin with these letters. This type of search could include words beginning with 'shoe...'.

  Type the word you are looking for and place a * immediately after, i.e. "shoe*". This will find items containing words such as shoelace, shoehorn, shoestring, shoetree, etc.

1. Search for items where the seller will accept **PayPal**.

    By ticking this box, only items which list PayPal as a payment option will be displayed. PayPal is very easy for buyers and many prefer to use it. eBay have included this search as they own PayPal and charge the seller a fee to offer PayPal as a payment means.

2. Search for items within a certain **time frame**.

    There are two boxes towards the end of the advanced search options that allow you to search for listings and stipulate the time frame that they are in. For example, you could search for listings that started within the last three hours, or that will end in the next three days. Perhaps the most interesting of the advanced search options is the 'Completed Listings Only'.

    For this search, you will need to sign into eBay. As before, enter your search words into the box and now tick 'Completed Listings Only'. The results shown will be for all of the auctions which ended in the past 30 days containing your search words. This list will also contain items that did not sell.

    As a seller it is very important to know how popular an item is likely to be before you buy 500 of them from your wholesaler. This search should help you with your wholesale buying.

NOTE eBay shops have their own unique internet address. Items within these shops will be included in searches made by search engines such as Google. I will explain this further when we look at eBay shops in more detail.

How to find other eBay users

There will be times when you will want to find out more information about another eBay user. You may have been asked about a postal rate, but the user forgot to tell you where they are in the world. You may also want to find out more about a user's trading record when considering the removal of their bid.

The eBay advanced search facility will allow you to trace other users and find out a little more about them. The process is much the same as a search for items. Start by accessing the Advanced Search screen; there is a small sub-menu on the left side of the page with half a dozen search options available. There are really only three you will need:

1.   Find a member;

2.   Find items by seller; and

3.   Find items by bidder.

These are described in more detail below.

1. Find a member

To find a member, or user, just click on the link and type their eBay ID into the search box and click search. Just in case you type it incorrectly, eBay will provide any near matches for your search. When the results are shown, just click on the user name and their profile details will appear.

Fig 4. Member profile

This profile will show the user's trading history, feedback score and how long they have been a member. As a seller, you are more likely to be interested in their location, if they make regular bid retractions, how many negative feedbacks they have and what they were for. As a general rule, the higher number of feedbacks a person has, the more likely they are to complete a trade with no problems. These users know how the system works and will not want to jeopardise a high score by defaulting on a purchase. Inexperienced bidders can require a little more assistance during the trade, which is why you will sometimes see sellers who do not take bids from new eBay users.

>
> **NOTE** Some countries, such as Germany, have strict rules about the disclosure of personal information. Profile information is not made available until you/buyers actually enter into a trade.

2. Find items by seller

This search will find all of the items listed by a specific seller and is great for checking on the competition.

The 'find items by seller' search works in much the same way as the 'find member' search. There is an extra option: the ability to include completed listings during the past month.

Type in the seller's eBay ID, click the 'Include completed listings' box and all the current auctions and any that ended within the month will be displayed.

Fig 5. Find items by seller

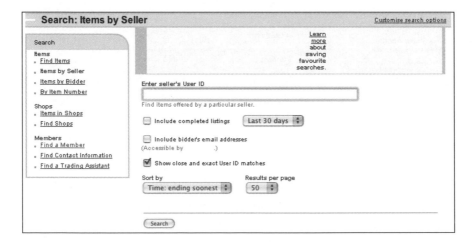

>
> **TIP** Use this search to see how the market is performing for other sellers. If your competitors are selling the same items, consider holding back for a while.

3. Find items by bidder

In the same way as the above search, it is also possible to search for the items that a particular buyer is bidding on. You can also select the items that they bid on during the last month. As a seller you may need to discover if a bidder is serious about your item. Are they an avid collector with a track record of purchases in this area?

This search will also show if the bidder went on to win the item and who the seller is.

TIP Use this search to track your competitor's buying activity. If they buy and sell through the same ID, you can see if they have found an item of interest and perhaps go on to bid against them and win the item yourself. Let other people do your research for you, follow their bidding activity and then outbid them at the last minute.

What to look for when searching

As you search through eBay, imagine yourself in the position of a buyer. How do you feel when you see other seller's auctions, would you bid? The key to successful selling is to try and understand things from the buyer's point of view. It is not enough to believe that you have the best looking auctions and that everything is just great, if, for some reason, buyers do not agree.

Most sellers on eBay will not have given this subject much consideration, they will just list their auction without too much thought as to how it looks to their customers. With some planning about the whole environment that you create, you will soon be far ahead of the competition.

TIP When looking at an auction, make notes of things you like and the things that don't work as well as they should. Decide for each item that you look at if you would in fact trade with the seller. Record your first impressions as these are seldom wrong.

Below are just some of the areas that will be of interest and might just help with the design of your own auctions.

Content

Check the content of the auctions you visit: How is the seller actually promoting their item? Does the content of the auction include the seller's terms and conditions? Is the description of the item comprehensive or does it consist of only a few sparse details? Do you feel that the seller cares about the item or is it just another business transaction?

TIP Check the feedback score of the sellers you find. Is there a difference in the way that experienced sellers present their items as opposed to sellers with less sales to their name?

Load time

A key factor in making a successful auction is striking a balance between the amount of content that is included, against the amount of time it takes to load the page. The advent of broadband in the UK will eventually make the load time of a page irrelevant, but until it reaches every home, it remains a concern. Not every country will have broadband, so load time remains an issue for international sellers.

> I have decided to cater for bidders with both broadband and traditional dial-up connections. Most of my auctions have just one large picture and links to additional information. Visitors who are particularly interested can access this information and are more likely to wait for the extra pages to load.

Terms and conditions

Many sellers include their terms and conditions within each listing – you will see many different formats as you search. Look also at the tone in which these are presented. Does the seller have hard and fast rules about payment within a certain period of time and do they threaten consequences if you do not meet these terms? Some sellers will leave negative feedback after 7 days if payment is not received. How does this make you feel about trading with these sellers? Other sellers insist that you have a certain number of feedbacks before you bid or will ask that you

> I will not trade with a seller who has created a hostile environment, it is just not a nice place to do business.

contact them before placing a bid. Again, how do you feel about this?

Give some thought to the type of conditions you will apply to your site and also decide how you will present them to your potential buyers.

TIP When selling on eBay, you must anticipate how bidders are going to find your item. Imagine yourself in their position, how would you search for your items?

Top tips for successful searches

1. Use different combinations of search words.
   Imagine which words a seller might use to describe their item. Try several different phrases and combinations.

2. For an even more precise search, state the brand/colour/model of the item.
   To find a 1980s model of R2D2 from the Star Wars films, your search could be: "Star Wars R2D2 1980 Lucas Films"

3. Search titles and descriptions to get more matches.
   You will get more results by searching in title and description. There are only 55 characters of space in the title box, so sellers often cannot fit all of the keywords in and will add them into the description.

4. Add or remove the letter 's' for more results.
   You will see two different lists of items when you search for cup and cups. Try your search with and without the final 's'.

5. Punctuate correctly.
   Punctuation marks, such as "–" in T-shirt should only be included in the search if you expect it to be in the item description.

Establish your selling account

Once you have an idea of what you would like to sell in your auctions, it is time to create your eBay selling account.

You may already have an eBay account as a buyer, you may already sell on eBay, or eBay may be completely new. This section will look in more detail at:

1.   Your eBay name that you will use for selling;

2.   the types of account; and

3.   how to set up a seller's account from the beginning.

Choosing a name

Selecting your eBay ID is the hardest part of the registration process, as most of the names you will think of have already been taken. It is, however, the most vital element – creating a trading name that meets the following criteria should ensure greater sales success.

1.   **Name length**
      When a bidder wants to search for you by name, maybe just to browse your items, they will need to type your name into the search engines The longer your name, the more likely they are to make a mistake when typing and never reach your site at all.

2.   **Format**
      Keep the format easy to type, and remember: hyphens are often forgotten; underscores require two keys to be pressed; and numbers are awkward to remember.

3.   **Memorable**
      Make your name memorable. Try to construct a name that can be pronounced – the most obvious names have been taken, but with some thought you should be able to arrive at something. A jumble of letters and numbers, maybe initials and a date of birth, such as BGH121070, will not be remembered and we want to make sure as many satisfied customers as possible come back to buy again.

4.   Relevant

If you intend to focus on a specific area of sales, try to make your name relevant to the market. You may already have found some sellers who have the item they sell within their name, examples might include *Nokiaman, Batteryseller, DVDshop* and so on. (I have just made these up to illustrate how a name can reflect the sales activity.)

The beginning of a brand

Your trading name will form the beginning of your brand identity. Changing it at a later date is possible, but should be avoided to ensure that your existing customers can find you in the future. You may decide to incorporate your name onto stationary, packing slips, address labels, email signatures, etc, even advertising in the future.

Top five things to consider when choosing a name

1   **Keep it short**
Make your name easy for bidders to type. Don't make them re-write War and Peace just to find you.

2.   **Only use letters**
Avoid using numbers in your name, letters are easier to remember.

3.   **Spell out a word**
Make your name into something that can be pronounced, a jumble of letters won't be remembered.

4.   **Avoid current trends**
Choose a name that won't date. Avoid topical films and other subjects that won't mean as much in a few years time.

5.   **Consider more than one account**
Establish separate accounts for each product area you sell in and maybe another as a buying account.

Creating an account

Having chosen a trading name, the next stage is to set up a trading account on eBay.

Your selling account will operate from your 'My eBay' page, which can be accessed from the top menu that appears on every eBay page. All of your current sales activity will appear on this page – it can be regarded as your account dashboard.

From here you will be able to see how many items you are selling, how many sold and how many didn't. You can customise this view to show a trading period that best suits your needs.

Create a new selling account

The process to create a selling account is very straightforward.

1.   If you **already have an account as a buyer,** simply upgrade from your 'my eBay' section.

2.   If you are **starting from scratch,** go to the eBay home page and click on 'Register'. (See opposite Fig 6.)

The instructions are easy to follow. You will need to enter your personal contact details, email address, and so on. eBay will first create an account for you as a buyer, which you can then upgrade to a seller's account.

You will be asked for either a credit card number or your bank account details, or both. This is to ensure that eBay can collect their fees when you create your first auction. You will only have to enter these once.

There are no upfront charges and you will not need to deposit any money with eBay. [Fees are discussed in much more detail in a later section.] You can monitor your account status and see how much money you owe eBay in fees by clicking on the 'seller account' link on the 'My eBay' page at any time.

Fig 6. Registration page

Private Registration: Enter Information   Help

1 Enter Information   2. Choose User ID & Password   3. Check Your Email

Register now to bid, buy or sell on any eBay site. It's easy and free! Already Registered?

Your privacy is important to us

Account Type
Private Account
Change to Business Account

We do not sell or rent your personal information to third parties for their marketing purposes without your explicit consent.

Business sellers should register with a business account. Learn more about business registration.

To learn more, see eBay's privacy policy.

First name   Last name

Street address

Town / City

County   Post code   Country
-- Select County --   United Kingdom

Primary telephone   Secondary telephone (Optional)
(   )   (   )
Example: (020) 12316670 Needed if there are questions about your account

Date of Birth
--Day--   --Month--   --Year--
You must be at least 18 years old to use eBay

Important: A working email address is required to complete registration.
Email address

Examples: myname@aol.com or myname@yahoo.com
Re-enter email address

eBay's User Agreement and Privacy Policy
In order to use eBay, you must first read and agree to eBay's User Agreement. These are the terms and conditions that apply to your use of eBay. eBay's User Agreement can be viewed and printed by clicking here.

You should also read eBay's Privacy Policy to learn about the ways in which we use and protect your personal information. The Privacy Policy can be viewed and printed by clicking here.

By checking the boxes below, I confirm the following:
☐ I have read and accept the User Agreement and I have read the Privacy Policy.
☐ I agree to receive communications from eBay and understand that I can change my notification preferences at any time in My eBay.
☐ I must be an adult (18 years old) to trade on eBay and I certify that I am an adult and can enter into this Agreement.

Use an existing account

You can of course use an existing account to sell through, as well as buy with. This can be a good idea if you already have a high feedback score as some sales facilities only become available with a certain rating. If your feedback as a buyer is not that good, create a new account and start afresh.

If you're selling *and* buying on eBay

Give some thought as to where you may acquire stock in the future. If you intend to buy from eBay and then sell it back via eBay [which is something we will look at later in greater detail], a separate buyer's account might be a good idea.

> I have several eBay accounts; one for buying, with the others used for selling different types of item. This allows me to offer specific items through a dedicated ID rather than have everything sold through a general account.

This will avoid the situation where your buying and selling activity can be viewed within the same account. For one, it might upset the person you bought the items from to see them turned round and sold on for a healthy profit.

TIP   Consider re-naming your account. Perhaps the single most important aspect to successful eBay selling is the name that you trade with. It is your brand identity and the name that bidders will search for if they want to check your site again.

To change your eBay ID, access the 'A-Z' help screen, type in 'change user ID' and then click on 'changing your user ID'.

Auction design

Now that we have completed some research into eBay, chosen a trading name and created our selling account, it is time to give some thought as to how we would like our auctions to look. By working through some ideas before you start to sell, the auctions will have a consistency of appearance. Although the look will no doubt change over time, the basics will be in place.

Having an appealing design layout for your auctions is more likely to entice the visitor to place a bid. In a pleasant, well thought out environment, placing a bid will become more enjoyable. Imagine you are in a high street shop with very loud music, a very loud colour scheme and a jumble of information at every turn. This may be the type of shop that appeals to you, or it may in fact deter you from staying to browse their products. An eBay auction is exactly the same. Design the layout and content for your target customers and they will return.

It is possible to alter the appearance of almost anything within the auction, so you will see variations on the listings you look at. Some auctions have borders around the edge, different colour backgrounds, moving text or pictures, multiple pictures and so on. Maybe you will discover a site design that really appeals to you and gives you ideas for your own site.

The section below will touch on some of the areas of site design that can be changed. I will show in more detail in a later section how this is done but, for now, give some thought as to how you would like your auctions to look.

Page format

This is not intended to be a technical section, but a plan of how you want the finished site to look and feel. Some of the elements may require a little more technical knowledge and we will address many aspects of this in later sections of the book.

Background colour

The standard background colour is white. You may be happy with this or wish to try something else. Don't worry about how the look will be achieved at this time, we will cover the processes later.

Text colour

The default text colour is black. Depending on what you decide to do with the background colour, the text colour may need to be changed.

Text size

The size of text is something that varies from seller to seller – you may have already noticed this. It is easy to alter text size and larger text does have obvious advantages, but if the description is very detailed, larger text will make the page very long and a little difficult to read. It may be worth considering the use of titles within the description layout and adding weight to keywords and phrases.

Templates

The basic auction template has been constructed by eBay. It is essentially a blank space within which you can enter the description of your item. It is possible to use custom templates which are available from the internet, and to then copy them into your auction. These templates may have a cost associated with them, or some other requirements, such as credits to the author, which will need to be incorporated.

In a later section I will demonstrate how to create your own template using basic HTML code; this will allow you to fully customise your auctions. If, however, you would prefer to use an existing template, check out some of the sites below.

- *Alou Web Design* (www.alouwebdesign.ca/free-ebay-templates.htm) Currently offers 20 free eBay templates and a host of other design tools.

- *Auction Insights* (auctioninsights.com/practice/auction-template.html) Has a free online auction creator, just fill in the blanks and your eBay listing will appear.

- *Auction Supplies* (auctionsupplies.com/templates/) Has the code for a number of templates, just copy and paste it into the description of your listing.

- *Web Craft Creations* (www.webcraftscreations.com/web-design/ebay-web-site-design.html) Offers customised template designs, with costs starting at about £200.

The nature of general internet pages means that not all options will be available for your eBay description area; the main page specifics will have set some of the parameters for your space. If you are thinking of using an external template, check first that it will work on eBay.

TIP When starting to sell on eBay, stick with the basic template and consider altering it as your experience grows.

Pictures

Having great pictures in your auctions will certainly help push the prices higher. Even here, eBay gives you some options: how many pictures you will include, how big you want them and where the picture sits within your auction.

Picture size

eBay allow the first picture to be loaded into your auction for no charge. This will be a standard size of 400 x 300 pixels. For an additional fee you can show this picture in a larger size. The fee structure is fully explained in a later section, but for now, give some thought as to the size of picture you would like to use.

Multiple pictures

Some items are perfect for extra pictures: collectables, china, models, etc will often be shown both back and front as the bidder will want to see the overall condition. Extra pictures will certainly help to sell these items.

> I am very keen on extra pictures and would recommend that at least two are used. I will show you how to include these extra pictures for no additional cost in a later section, but for now, decide if your auctions should have more than one.

Consider also items such as DVDs, CDs or computer games where there is a comprehensive description or track listing on the back of the case or box. To save time copying these out, just take a second picture so that the bidder can read the detail directly from the packaging.

Close up pictures will sell items. They suggest that the seller has nothing to hide, and being prepared to show the item in close up will encourage higher bidding.

TIP When using close up pictures, include a ruler or coin to give an idea of scale. If selling overseas, use a Euro coin and maybe an American one as these will be familiar to the bidders.

One of my favourite eBay stories (apparently completely true) relates to a seller of shoes receiving an email that said:

> *"You list the shoes as a size 6, but are they really a size 6, they look like a size 7. I wondered if there might be an error in the description?"*

Picture location

The location of the picture is one of the most important elements of the whole auction. Pictures at the top of the listing will catch the viewer's eye and convince them to read further about the item.

Links to additional pages

In your auction description it is possible to include certain links to other internet sites. I will explain how this is achieved in a later section, but at this design stage, consider the use of some of these links as they will provide your bidders with extra information. This will also reduce your workload as some frequently asked questions can be answered by following these links.

eBay have very strict rules concerning the use of external links from within auctions, but, as a general rule, if the destination site only offers information, it will be allowed.

I have listed below a few examples of links that you may consider for your own auctions. This is not an exhaustive list, but remember we want the bidder to stay focused on buying our product and not wandering too far from the auction. Send them to an information site by all means, but do not make your destination link more interesting than your own auction or they might forget to bid.

Currency converters

There are several currency converters on the internet and it is possible to provide direct links to them – although there is also a currency converter within eBay. Providing a link to a converter will reduce the number of questions you receive from overseas bidders regarding currency exchange rates. Some of the best currency converters I have found are:

- Bloomberg (www.bloomberg.com/analysis/calculators/currency.html)

- Yahoo Finance (finance.yahoo.com/currency)

- Oanda.com (www.oanda.com/convert/classic)

All currency converters work in the same way. eBay operates it's own at pages.ebay.co.uk/services/buyandsell/currencyconverter.html. To use a converter, just type in the quantity that needs to be converted (e.g. 27.78), then select the type of currency that you have (e.g. UK pounds – often referred to as GBP) and then the currency that you want to convert into (e.g. US Dollars).

Language translators

As with currency converters, there are several language translation sites available on the internet, and many of these are free. Although they may not translate perfectly, they are more than adequate to provide a good understanding of what is for sale. Two of the language converters I use most frequently are:

- Altavista Bablefish (babelfish.altavista.com/babelfish/tr)

- Free Translation (www.freetranslation.com)

To use the translator, just write in English the phrase you want to translate, select the 'to' and 'from' languages and click enter.

 TIP When using a translation service to construct a reply to an overseas enquiry, use simple phrases that are grammatically correct; this will increase the chances of a good translation.

Postal sites

A direct link to the Royal Mail website or another carrier site will demonstrate to your customers that your postage rates are not high (and they can check if they wish). This may also save time as bidders can check any issues relating to insurance and delivery times themselves and they should email you less. I have included a comprehensive list of postal services in a later section along with some internet references.

Links to your other auctions

It's great if visitors to your site can see a selection of your other items on the same page that might appeal to them. There are a number of ways of achieving this:

1.   Firstly, you could just mention in your description that you have other items for sale and hope that the visitor checks them out. If selling a pair of hiking boots for example, you could write something along the lines: 'If these boots are just what you are looking for, please check our other auctions where you will also find a great backpack and selection of walking sticks.' To see these items, the potential customer would have to visit your 'items for sale' page and then click on the auction for the walking sticks.

2.   The next option would be to have a similar statement about your items and also place a link directly to your 'items for sale' page next to it. This would remove one step. eBay have already created this link for you, it is just waiting to be used. eBay call this an 'insert', and I will explain it fully later in the book.

3.   The third way would be to make part of your statement into a direct link to the actual auction. So in the phase we used above, the actual words 'backpack' and 'walking sticks' will become clickable links, taking your customer directly to the auction. This option does involve some knowledge of HTML codes, but it is fully explained later in the book.

4.   The last method I will mention at this point is very similar to the above; still with a statement containing clickable links, but this time with a small picture of the actual item appearing alongside. This means your bidder can see the walking sticks, click on the picture and be taken to the auction.

These cross-selling techniques will drive your sales higher and can be used to increase the number of visits to an item that is not performing very well.

> I use two direct links to additional auctions on each of my listings and use them to cross-sell my items, trying at all times to keep potential bidders within my range of auctions.

Links to pages containing additional content and pictures

It may be useful to have links within your listings that refer the visitor to an extra web page for additional pictures and your general terms and conditions. This will help with the load time of your main auction page and remove some clutter from the actual auction.

Linking to these extra web pages is a little more advanced and is covered in the later section concerning the development of your auctions.

TIP Only include supplementary information on additional pages as not everybody will click through to them and the visitor may miss your key messages.

The eBay linking policy – what is and is not allowed

eBay have very strict rules about what kind of links can be placed within the auction description. For a full breakdown, click on the 'Links policy' from the help pages.

Links allowed

In summary, these are the links that are currently allowed:

- One link to a page that **further describes the item** being sold in that listing.

- One link to **your email address** for potential buyers to ask questions about the item in that listing.

- Links to **photos** of the item for sale.

- Links to **your eBay auctions** (including your eBay Shop).

- Links to your **'About Me' page** (which I will explain in the next section).

- Links that provide **credits** to third parties.

- One link to your listing **terms and conditions.**

Links not allowed

There are certain links that are *not* allowed. The below is not a comprehensive list, but does indicate the kind of links in question.

- Links to web pages that offer to trade, sell or purchase **goods or services outside of eBay.** This applies whether it is a static URL or an active link.

- Links to websites or pages offering merchandise is **not permitted on eBay.**

- Links to sites that **solicit eBay User IDs or passwords** from buyers.

- Links that encourage buyers to **place their eBay bids through a site other than eBay.**

TIP If in any doubt about whether you can use a particular link, just email the eBay support team and ask them.

The 'About Me' page

eBay provides users with an extra page known as the 'About Me' page, which can be used to tell other users more about them. Although it is not a direct part of your individual auctions, it can be used alongside your listings and form part of your overall design.

You can add anything to this page: a little about yourself, why you love eBay, your favourite hobbies, etc. If you are using eBay to make money, this is also an ideal location to further sell yourself and your items.

Very few people have an 'About Me' page; you can see who has by the blue and red 'me' symbol after their feedback number.

This has to be a good idea. It is free and I have 1,000 hits per month to mine – that's 1,000 people looking at what I have to say, viewing all of my auctions on one page, checking out my recent feedback and maybe clicking on a few links to my auctions.

TIP When it comes to the design of your About Me page, check out other pages and see what could work for you. Do not copy them, but adapt and take the best elements from several pages.

This page as an aid to sales

Using this free page to tell people what your favourite television programme is or other similar things is very entertaining, but may not drive up your sales all that much. If someone takes the trouble to visit your About Me page, use this visit to push your sales higher: outline your terms and conditions; make the page friendly; list some of the other fantastic items that you will soon be selling; and create links to other pages.

TIP When you create your About Me page, you have the option to show your most recent feedbacks, which is always a good idea if they are positive. You can also show up to 100 of your current items for sale, which means that a visitor can see 100 on one page; whereas when viewing the traditional 'items for sale' page, they would have to click through four pages. The fewer the number of clicks, the better.

What to include and why

Include the details of your terms and conditions – tell the visitor what they need to know in order to trade with you. Placing this information on the About Me page will keep your auctions free of confusing detail. Just place a note and a hyperlink from your listings to this page.

By all means tell the visitor why you love eBay so much. Make it personal to a degree, and you will begin to create a relationship with your potential bidders. The general belief is that people buy from people; capitalise on this by including things that show you as a real person.

Outline anything that you feel will set you apart from other sellers. Maybe your speed of dispatch or quality of packaging. Use the page to convince the bidder that you are the person to do business with.

 TIP If you modify the format of your auction pages at a later date (e.g. change the colour scheme), continue the theme onto your About Me page to give a sense of continuity.

Further links to additional pages

The eBay rules concerning external links to other sites are more relaxed on an About Me page, so take advantage of them; provide links to currency converters, language translators and the Post Office site for postage rates.

All this helps to demonstrate to potential buyers that you have given careful thought to your service, and that you are a serious seller.

I decided to go one stage further with my About Me page and now have my trading terms and conditions in four additional languages: French, German, Spanish and Italian. The quality of the translation is not perfect, but it does show a willingness to try and be part of Europe. I created these extra pages, which are hosted on my own website, as part of a sales push into Europe – it can only have helped. Whilst this may seem a little too much at this time, it does show the kind of thing that this page can be used for.

External web space

If you have some internet web space already, it is possible to use that to host additional pages for your auctions. You may have some web space available through your Internet Service Provider (ISP), or you may pay for it. Either way, this additional space is a great way to present information to your customers without having too much detail on your item listings.

If you don't already have web space of your own, but would like to look into it further, check out these sites:

- **50 Megs** (www.50megs.com)

  This site offers a range of services including free hosting space to get you started. To get enough space, you will need to pay for the service. A good package is the 'Starter Plus' and costs $3.32 per month, that's about £1.70. The package includes:

  50MB Web space

  2GB of Bandwidth

  5MB File size

- Bravenet (www.bravenet.com)

  This provider also offers a free package and two other main options. The 'Basic Hosting Package' costs $5.95 per month, about £3.30. It includes the following:

  30GB of bandwidth

  1,000MB disk space

  30 email accounts

  Free domain name

  30 sub domains

  500+ FREE site templates

 TIP Check that your site will allow pictures stored on It to be viewed on eBay; the free services may not allow this.

I currently use 50Megs to host my pictures along with a number of other web pages that I have built. This service costs me about £4 per month and I have 100MB of storage space. To save money on increased storage, I will delete pictures from my website as auctions end.

Personal or business-like?

The decision to make your auctions formal or informal will depend very much upon your own style and the items you are going to sell. There is no hard and fast rule. As you look through other eBay auctions, you will see examples of both styles. Use the method you feel most comfortable with.

> Right from the very beginning I decided to make my auctions as informal as possible. There are no strict deadlines about payment or who is allowed to bid; I believe that this approach works well for my type of business.

Decide on your target market

One of the biggest decisions when selling on eBay is to decide how large you would like your target market to be. The world seems a very big and complicated place, and it is much more comfortable to sell only to the UK as it is a place you know.

> When I first started to sell, it was only to the UK. I had many emails from international bidders asking me to sell to them, which is a fantastic position to be in, but I said no. Just how much money was lost in those early days I will never know. I now sell 40% of my items overseas.

There are some things that you would not want to sell overseas. They may be too heavy, too tricky to pack, even the amount of payment clearing fees could be a consideration.

Overview of the eBay selling zones

eBay will let you choose your marketplace. There is a comprehensive set of options during the listing process and you can change your options for different auctions. The pros and cons of the various marketplaces are listed opposite.

UK only

Advantages

- The UK is a familiar place
- No language concerns
- Next day delivery is possible
- You can agree local pickup or delivery
- Weight and packing considerations are well known

Within the UK the postage costs are very clear and we are all familiar with the way the Post Office works; we understand the way that parcels should be sent. Sending mail overseas is something that we may not have done before.

Disadvantages

- A limited market
- More competition from UK only sellers
- Sale price may be compromised

There is no doubt that an auction that is available to a larger audience will attract more bids and is also likely to reach a higher sale price.

Europe

Advantages

- Larger potential customer base than just the UK
- Fewer customs restrictions than trading worldwide

Disadvantages

- Weight and packing requirements are different
- Delivery time (air mail/surface mail)
- Currency considerations (not always the Euro)
- Language considerations

Global

Advantages

- The largest marketplace of all

Disadvantages

- Customs clearance
- Shipping requirements and insurance
- Payment options are limited
- Multiple currency options
- Language considerations
- Returns are more complicated

TIP   Sell to the world, make your potential market as big as possible, it really is very easy.

The first item I sold outside of the UK was a music CD to Canada. It happened by accident. At the time I was only selling in the UK and had no idea of what would be involved in shipping to the world. But the highest bidder was in Canada, so I had to learn the process at the end of the auction, or lose the sale. I learnt very quickly and opened all my auctions to the world the next day.

What to consider when choosing your target market

When choosing your market it is important to complete your research and market your products accordingly. How you actually design your site to address this market will depend on the product and the countries you wish to sell into. Here are just a few areas which may well be worth considering early on:

1. **The weight of your items**
   The more your item weighs, the higher the postage charges will be. This may make it too much for overseas bidders to buy, and will restrict your market and profit margin.

2. **Operating and legal restrictions**

   Some countries will have different restrictions on what can be sent. If you intend to market a particular product overseas, check to see if it is permitted.

3. **Money transfer fees**

   When using electronic money systems, such as PayPal, you will be charged a fee depending upon the total value of the money transferred – *including* the postage. As overseas buyers are likely to pay using this type of method, you will pay more in fees as the postage will be higher.

Establish your trading terms and conditions

Setting out how you will do business seems such an obvious thing to do, as it will make the whole transaction much easier if the buyer knows what to expect. However, it's surprising just how many eBay sellers do not include this information. Deciding how you will trade before you start should ensure that every one of your transactions has a good chance of a successful conclusion.

As a seller, you will have considerable control over your auction and can impose almost any conditions you see fit. The following are just some of the areas where you will have control:

- Which areas of the world you will do business with

- Who pays for postage costs, including any insurance premiums

- Which postal services you will offer

- How long it will be before you post the item

- How long you will allow buyers to pay

- Which payment methods you will accept

- Whether you will sell to buyers with less than, say, 10 feedbacks

- You can block any eBay user you don't want to trade with

You can decide how you will trade and the buyer must fall in line with you or you can refuse to complete the trade. I would just make a note of caution at this point: the harder your trading terms are, the fewer bidders you are likely to attract. It is a balancing act.

I have included a typical T&C statement in the appendices, which you might like to use as a basis for creating your own.

How and where to display your T&C

How you tell your visitors about your terms and conditions (T&C) of trading will depend upon the final layout of your auction listings. You may decide to have them on your About Me page and refer visitors to them, or you may wish to have them attached to each auction, or on a separate internet page via an interactive link.

> After much consideration I decided to keep my actual auctions as short as possible and have my trading terms on my About Me page. I feel that it keeps my page load time low and does not distract my buyers from the actual item for sale.

Create a pleasant environment

When writing your T&C, try not to be too aggressive – make your point, but word it in such a way that a visitor will not feel intimidated. If you require payment within 7 days, explain why (maybe you have had several non-payers). If you will not accept bids from new members, ask them to email you for help and assistance rather than stating that they cannot bid. Remember, people buy from people.

What to include in the T&C

Exactly what you decide to include within your T&C will depend on the kind of customers you want to sell to, and where in the world they are. It is quite likely that you will change these conditions over time as you gain an insight into the kind of problems that can occur. There are a few standard terms that you may wish to consider from the beginning:

- postage terms;

- returns policy; and

- payments policy.

These three key areas are discussed below.

1. Postage terms

Setting out your postage terms before you list your auctions will ensure that all your customers will know what to expect. Once the auction has ended, the winning bidder will want the item as soon as possible – it is, after all, the prize they were bidding for.

 TIP Provide all postage rates in advance, and Buyers will know exactly what the total costs are. This will reduce the number of questions and therefore save time.

How often you will post

Some sellers will only post on certain days of the week. This will cut down on trips to the Post Office, but will lead to delays in delivery. If you intend to clear funds before you dispatch the item, include these timescales so that your buyer can anticipate when to expect the item. How you intend to send the item will also impact on the delivery time; again, put the postal services you offer into your postage terms.

Proof of postage

The Post Office will cover most items for a minimum amount should it become lost or damaged whilst in their system. However, this is not always the case and should not be relied on. There is a standard proof of postage form which can be completed and stamped by the Post Office at the time of dispatch.

 TIP Always obtain a proof of postage. It's free and will provide you with a chance of recovering some money should an item not arrive.

Which postal services you will offer

As we will see when we look at listing your first auction, you will be able to offer three domestic UK postal services and state the appropriate costs. There is a pull down menu of options; just select the one you need for each postal service. The list currently includes:

UK postal options	International postal options
Royal Mail 1st Class standard	Royal Mail Airmail
Royal Mail 2nd Class standard	Royal Mail Airsure
Royal Mail 1st class recorded	Royal Mail Surface mail
Royal Mail 2nd class recorded	Royal Mail International Signed for
Royal Mail special delivery	Royal Mail HM Forces Mail
Royal Mail Standard Parcels	Parcelforce International Datapost
ParcelForce 24	Parcelforce Ireland 24
ParcelForce 48	Parcelforce Euro 48
Other courier	Parcelforce International Scheduled
Collection in person	Other courier or delivery service
	Collect in person

From the choice of postal services that you offer for your item, the winning bidder can choose the method that suits them best. The more options you can offer the bidder, the more likely they may be to bid.

Include any specific postage requirements (e.g. insurance)

You may decide that your successful bidders will have to pay for insurance. If so, state this in your T&C and include it in the relevant section within each auction. The prices for insurance will vary according to the value of the item; again the details will be on the Royal Mail website at www.royalmail.com or available from your chosen courier service.

Liability statement

It is quite common for eBay sellers to state that the posting of an item cannot guarantee delivery, and that the liability for a lost parcel lies with the buyer. If you have a 'proof of posting', then you may choose to assist the buyer is tracking down a lost item (this just involves filling in a form). If compensation is not made, state that you, the seller, are not held responsible.

Multiple purchases

Will you offer a reduction in postage costs for multiple purchases? This may save you packing time and may also encourage bidders to buy more items.

2. Returns policy

Having a returns policy will provide your bidders with the confidence that should anything not be as expected, they can return the item. This should increase the number of bids you receive, but give some serious thought as to the wording you use so that returning an item is the last resort for a buyer. Here are just a few things to consider when setting out your returns policy:

- Will you refund the postage as well as the item cost?

- How long will you allow for a bidder to return an item?

- What grounds will you accept for a refund?

 TIP Don't make your returns policy too easy for the bidders or you may find that you are always getting things sent back. You are in this to make money, not offer a 'try before you buy' service!

3. Payments policy

When setting a payments policy, you may decide that you will accept different payment options from different countries. I will discuss the alternatives for receiving payment in more detail in the next section, along with some costs for each service. When deciding upon a payments policy, you may consider having one for UK customers and another for international buyers, based upon the costs of each service.

How long will you allow before payment should be received?

Just how long you will wait before chasing for payment is an important decision. It may depend on the value of the item, or the feedback history of the buyer. Each case may be different. However, having a general rule will let the buyer know what is expected of them.

> I am quite relaxed about payment timescales as I trade with many new eBay members, and am prepared to wait a little longer. I will wait for one week before sending a polite email asking if all is OK and then if there is no reply after a further week, I will send a reminder through the 'Non Paying Buyer' process (explained later).

Payment clearance times

For a payment option that takes some time to clear, such as a personal cheque, state how long it will be before you send the item. Cheques clear in about 5 working days, so just put this into your trading terms. Electronic cheques also take some time to clear (although they can arrive via the PayPal system), and should be treated as traditional cheques.

Payment options

Deciding which payment options to accept can have a big impact on your eBay business. Should you accept electronic payments in addition to cheques, bank transfers, or perhaps even international cheques?

In this section I have listed some of the more popular payments methods that you could accept. You must decide which methods best suit your business needs.

The payment options are:

1. Online payment
2. Cash
3. Credit cards
4. Bank deposit
5. Personal cheques
6. Instant money transfer
7. Postal orders

These are explained below.

1. Online payment

Receiving money via the internet has grown in popularity over the last few years and it is now quite unusual to find an eBay seller that does not accept at least one form of electronic payment.

There are many companies offering to handle your money for a fee, of which the main company is PayPal. The most suitable system to use will depend upon the size of your organisation and the facilities you need to deploy. Below, I describe PayPal as well as a couple of other services: Nochex and WorldPay.

For larger volume businesses, possibly the cheapest method would be to use your own merchant account with your bank that will allow you to accept payments from the internet.

Smaller businesses may not require a full merchant account, and so could use either PayPal or Nochex, which are the most recognised names in what is becoming an overcrowded marketplace.

PayPal

PayPal.com is a web-based payment service, which enables consumers to send and receive money via their computer. PayPal is a truly global company; it currently has 71 million accounts in 45 countries.

PayPal can handle all of the major credit and debit cards and can access the banking infrastructure to enable funds to be deposited and withdrawn into your ordinary bank account.

It is a quick and easy way for businesses and entrepreneurs to accept credit card payments online without having to establish a merchant bank account to do so. PayPal enables any business or consumer with an email address to securely, conveniently and cost-effectively send and receive these payments.

PayPal is currently owned by eBay who purchased the company in October 2002.

A few quick facts about PayPal

- PayPal does not have a set up charge for either buyers or sellers and is available in 45 countries.

- There are mechanisms in place to protect the buyer and seller from fraud.

- Payments are made to your email address, which acts as an account ID number.

- The fee structure is easy to understand, but the fees may prove too expensive for some sellers.

- Sending money directly to another PayPal account is easy, and the transfer is very quick.

- Withdrawals can be made into your bank account, usually within 5 working days.

- Partial refunds can be made through the system, which will mean that if you refund some postage, for example, you will also recover some of the fees you paid on the original transaction.

- PayPal does have a range of merchant tools which may help your administration processes.

Some bidders will search for auctions that offer PayPal as a payment option. For the buyer, PayPal is very easy to use, the payment is instant and therefore their item can be sent that much quicker.

URL: www.paypal.com

Nochex

Nochex is an online payment system similar to PayPal that enables businesses and individuals trading online to accept instant, guaranteed, low cost payments, from anyone with a UK credit or debit card.

There are currently over 750,000 members, making Nochex the UK's largest email payment system.

How it works:

- Money is sent from either the sender's credit or debit card (they can also transfer money into their own Nochex account if they have one and then send it from there).

- The money is instantly moved from their bank account/credit card/Nochex account into the recipients Nochex account. Both parties will be notified by email that the money has been sent.

- Once the money has been sent, the recipient can withdraw it to their bank account. If they don't have a Nochex account they will need to register before they can withdraw the money.

URL: www.nochex.com

WorldPay

WorldPay is currently part of The Royal Bank of Scotland Group, which is the 5th biggest banking group in the world. WorldPay payment solutions are used by businesses both big and small. Customers of WorldPay can accept payments from Visa, MasterCard, Diners, American Express, and all the major credit cards. Debit cards can also be accepted, along with payment schemes such as Switch, Laser and Electron. These payments can be made in different currencies and in different languages.

URL: www.worldpay.com

Payment systems comparison

When looking at the costs of an online payments company, it is very difficult to compare like with like; much will depend upon your type of business and the amount of payments you receive online. The table overleaf makes some comparisons between the three most popular services, however this is presented for guidance only.

For a full comparison of the major online payments companies, visit the Department of Trade & Industry at www.electronic-payments.co.uk.

'Chargeback' is the term used by online payment companies when a buyer asks the credit card company to recover the payment, perhaps because the item was not delivered or a credit card was used fraudulently. The payment will be reversed out of your account back to the buyer.

Comparison of online payment companies	PayPal	Nochex	WorldPay
Set up fees	Zero	Zero	£75 to £100
Ongoing fees	Zero	Zero	£100 annually
Transaction fees	Sliding scale charges ranging from 1.9% to 3.4%, plus 20p per transaction.	2.5% plus an additional 20p per transaction.	4.5% of the total value of each transaction for credit cards and 50p for debit cards. They also take an additional 6p–10p for 'fraud protection'.
Customer registration	Required	Not required	Not required
Cash withdrawal	No charge for withdrawing more than £50, Less than £50, a 25p charge applies. Funds are transferred within 5 working days.	No charge for withdrawing more than £50, Less than £50, a 25p charge applies. Funds are transferred within 3–4 working days.	A 35p flat rate applies, and there is a four week delay before funds can be transferred.
Chargebacks	No fine for chargebacks, but funds may be frozen while dispute is settled.	A no chargebacks guarantee exists, protecting the merchant against fraudulent chargebacks.	£10 fine for each chargeback.

2. Cash

Cash is no longer permitted as a payment option on eBay as it is not traceable and there is no way to prove that the payment was received.

3. Credit cards

To accept credit card payments you will need the appropriate banking systems in place. For individuals this is not easy and can be costly. The majority of small sellers on eBay do not accept credit cards (a close substitute is PayPal).

4. Bank deposit

The ability for the buyer to deposit money directly into a bank account is great for sellers, as it is deposited as cash, and is therefore available straight away. Accepting money from another account in the UK is, as far as I am aware, free of any transaction costs. This is not necessarily the case when accepting money transfers from overseas.

To receive international payments you will need to obtain some details from your bank, these are known as IBAN and BIC or Swift codes. You will need to give these along with the name of your bank to your high bidder who will then make the transfer.

> I do not have many requests to accept international money transfers; if I do, I always ask the buyer to pay any associated fees.

5. Personal cheques

Personal cheques are still very common as a means of payment, especially by bidders who do not want an online account of any kind. Receiving a cheque is great as it can be deposited without any charges, unless you use a business account or deposit too many cheques. As your business grows, you may need to deposit cheques into a separate business account.

You can also accept personal cheques from overseas bidders that are drawn in other currencies. Depending on who you bank with, you will find that cheques up to a value of £30 can usually be exchanged for no charge; the banks negotiate them with each other. Offering to take personal cheques in other currencies may increase your international bids.

TIP If your item sells for more than £30, just ask the international bidder to send more than one cheque and then present them to your bank one at a time.

The exchange rate that you receive from your bank may not be that favourable and the money does take a while to be credited to your account. You will need to decide if this is worth offering as an additional payment option.

TIP When sending your invoice to your successful bidder, include a short note detailing who the cheque should be made payable to. I have had them made out to my user ID name, which proves very difficult to clear through the bank.

6. Instant money transfer

eBay are in the process of banning the use of instant money transfer as a means of payment. There have been instances of buyers sending money this way and then not receiving goods.

Weston Union is an example of an instant money transfer agent and has approximately 200,000 locations in 195 countries. Money can be transferred between these offices in a matter of minutes. There is a form to fill in for both the sender and receiver, and, depending upon the value of the transaction, identification may be required.

7. Postal orders

The traditional postal order is great for sellers as there are no fees for cashing them in; simply take them to your local Post Office and hand them over. The buyer will have to pay a fee when the postal order is purchased and this can be quite high depending on the number of orders.

The major drawback with postal orders comes as you may encounter delays at the Post Office when trying to cash them and time spent queuing is lost money.

TIP If you think that a buyer may be paying with a postal order and the item has a low price, offer them the alternative of sending ordinary postage stamps instead. They will save the postal order fees, you will not have to queue to cash the order and postage stamps are always useful.

Which payment options will you accept?

When you first start to sell, the variety of payment options available can seem quite confusing. The section below summarises a few of them and some of the advantages and disadvantages of each.

You can, of course, alter the payment methods that you accept for each auction. This can be a consideration if you sell a high value item, as the fees that you will incur could be quite large if the payment is made by a service such as PayPal.

Many sellers will have one set of payment methods for buyers within the UK, and another set of options for bidders outside of the UK. This mixture of payment method is a balance of ease of completion against the fees involved. One option would be to accept:

- traditional payment methods from bidders in the UK; and

- electronic payments from bidders throughout the rest of the world.

Payment methods	Benefits and risks
Bank deposit Buyer deposits payment directly into the seller's bank account either online or at most banks.	Not recommended. *Risks:* Payment is difficult to recover or cancel. Involves sharing personal account information.
Banker's draft A secure way of receiving money from someone you don't know. Commonly used for large purchases.	*Benefits:* Receipts are provided at the place of issue. Banker's drafts are usually traceable, but check with your bank. *Note:* Most banks charge the person requesting the draft to pay a fee. This fee could be more than the value of the item.
Cash	Not permitted. *Risks:* Not traceable. No way to prove payment was made. No protection against loss or theft in the mail. Not covered under eBay's Standard Purchase Protection Programme.
Credit cards Only accept credit cards if you have the systems in place to handle the payment.	Not recommended for small traders. *Benefits:* Traceable. Immediate and convenient. Limited liability: most credit card issuers provide online protection. *Note:* Debit card users may have less protection than credit card users for items that are not delivered, are defective, or have been misrepresented.
Escrow Recommended for high-price items.	*Benefits:* Payment is held by the escrow service until you receive and approve the item. For eBay transactions in the UK, you should only use the following eBay-approved escrow company: www.escrow.com

Instant money transfers (such as Western Union)	Not recommended and soon to be banned. eBay does not recommend the use of instant money transfer services. These services are designed to allow you to send money to family and friends – people you know and trust. *Risks:* Vulnerable to criminal misuse. Difficult to identify and designate recipient. Not traceable. Does not offer verification and cancellation privileges. Generally, no recourse is available if the item is not delivered as promised, even if you used your credit card to send the payment. Not covered under eBay's Standard Purchase Protection Programme.
PayPal Send and receive money using a credit card.	*Benefits:* Traceable. Immediate and convenient. Payment is deposited directly into the seller's account. Sellers don't see your credit card details (it's safely encrypted through PayPal's system), which limits the risk of unauthorised use. Automatic payment tracking. Covered up to £500 through PayPal's Buyer Protection Programme.
Personal cheque	*Benefits:* Traceable to a particular mailing address. Provides proof of payment. Covered by eBay and PayPal's Buyer Protection Programmes. Most banks offer a stop payment service if problems arise before the cheque is cashed (which may incur charges).
Postal Order An inexpensive way to send payments worldwide.	*Benefits:* Traceable to a particular mailing address. Easy to buy and cash at UK Post Offices. No bank account needed.

When it comes to receiving money, I will accept almost anything. The easier you make it for bidders to pay, the more likely you are to receive more bids and make more profit. I have found that bidders who have PayPal accounts, for example, prefer to use them, so I offer this facility on all of my auctions. Some bidders however would prefer not to pay electronically, so I also offer them a range of other payment methods.

Five tips to make receiving money easy

1. **Offer as many options as you can**

   Make it easy for your buyers to pay. The more options you offer, the more bids you will receive.

2. **Accept PayPal**

   It does cost money, but PayPal is now understood by most bidders and many will look for it as a payment option before bidding. Be selective on how you use it.

3. **Bank deposits**

   Obtain the information from your bank that will allow bank transfers from overseas. Ensure that the buyer pays any fees.

4. **Foreign personal cheques**

   Check with your bank and see if they will clear foreign cheques without making a charge. There is bound to be an upper limit, so include this in your trading terms.

5. **Clear funds before dispatch**

   It sounds like common sense, but ensuring the funds have cleared before you send the item will save a lot of time sorting out problems.

eBay charges

When managing any sales business, it is important to make a profit, and to buy stock that should sell well. It is also important to make enough money to cover all of your expenses and reward you for your time and effort. In a later section we will look more closely at bookkeeping, but, for now, give some thought as to the amount of money you want as a wage. Understanding the fee structure of eBay will help you calculate if the item you had in mind to sell is actually worth the trouble.

Current fee structure

The current fee structure of a standard eBay auction is basically split into two parts:

1. Insertion fee

2. Final value fee

These are described in some detail below.

1. Insertion fee

You will be charged a fee to actually place your auction onto the system. This *insertion fee* will depend on the price your auction will start at; at the time of writing, the range is between 15p and £2 for most auctions.

Table 1: Insertion fees

Starting or Reserve price	Insertion fee
£0.01 – £0.99	£0.15
£1.00 – £4.99	£0.20
£5.00 – £14.99	£0.35
£15.00 – £29.99	£0.75
£30.00 – £99.99	£1.50
£100 and above	£2.00

2. Final value fee

eBay will then also charge a percentage of the final sale price, the *final value fee*. This FVF works on a sliding scale method and is explained in the table below.

Table 2: Final value fees

Closing price	Final value fee
Item not sold	No fee.
£0.01 – £29.99	5.25% for the amount of the high bid (at the listing close for auction-style listings) up to £29.99.
£30.00 – £599.99	5.25% of the initial £29.99 (£1.57), plus 3.25% of the remaining closing value balance.
£600 and above	5.25% of the initial £29.99 (£1.57), plus 3.25% of the initial £30.00 – £599.99 (£18.53), plus 1.75% of the remaining closing value balance.

Optional feature fees

eBay will also offer you some optional upgrades to your basic listing design and for most of these, there is also a fee. I will expand on these services when we look in more detail about the actual listing procedure, but for now they will provide an idea of how the final cost of an auction is calculated. These optional feature fees have a fixed price and you can decide when you wish to use them. They currently include:

Reserve fees

Table 3: Reserve fees

Reserve price	Fee
£0.01 – £49.99	N/A
£50.00 – £4,999.99	2% of the reserve price
£5,000 and up	£100

Listing upgrade fees

Table 4: Listing upgrade fees

Feature	Fee	Feature	Fee
Gallery	£0.15	Highlight	£2.50
Listing Designer	£0.07	Featured Plus!	£9.95
Item Subtitle	£0.35	Gallery Featured	£15.95
Bold	£0.75	Home Page Featured	£49.95
Buy It Now	Variable	Scheduled Listings	6p
List in Two Categories	Double the insertion and listing upgrades fees (excluding Scheduled Listings and Home Page Featured).		

Picture service fees

Table 5: Picture service fees

Feature	Fee
First picture	Free
Each additional picture	12p
Picture show	15p
Super-size image	60p
Picture pack	1-6 pictures 90p / 7-12 pictures £1.35

Examples of eBay fees

Below are just a few examples of the breakdown of fees that might apply.

Table 6: Sale of music CD

eBay service	Fee
Basic listing fee with start price of 99p	15p
Gallery picture	15p
Final value fee with a sale price of £5.00	26p
Total cost of eBay fees	56p

Table 7: Sale of a computer

eBay service	Fee
Basic listing fee with start price of £200	£2.00
Gallery picture	15p
Final value fee with a sale price of £1,000	£27.10
Total cost of eBay fees	£29.49

Table 8: Sale of a mobile phone

eBay service	Fee
Basic listing fee with start price of £50	£1.50
Gallery picture	15p
Two extra pictures	24p
Super-size option	60p
Bold	75p
Highlight	£2.50
Featured Plus	£9.95
Final value fee with a sale price of £180	£6.44
Total cost of eBay fees	£22.13

eBay Motors

eBay also have fee structures for selling motor vehicles. Again you will pay an insertion fee and a final value fee (if the vehicle sells) to list a vehicle on eBay Motors. Currently there is a £6 insertion fee in place and an FVF scale as follows:

Table 9: Final value fee for motor vehicles

Closing price	Final Value Fee
£0.01 – £1,999.99	£15.00
£2,000.00 – £3,999.99	0.75%
£4,000.00 and above	£30.00

Other fees

In addition to the above eBay fees, money deposited into your account via an electronic method may also incur a fee. PayPal, for example, charges Premier and Business accounts to receive payments. Personal accounts are free, but may not receive credit or debit card payments. The fees are charged to your PayPal account and not your eBay account. More details on these charges will be given in the section concerning payment options.

Free listing days

On occasions, eBay will run promotions and will alter or suspend certain payment fees for a day. These take several forms and can result in a considerable saving if you are able to exploit them when they occur.

eBay do not give much notice when these promotions will run. However, they tend to be for auctions listed on a Thursday, which is a slow time, and you may only be notified by email on the preceding Tuesday. These are just a few of the variations that have been used:

- **Free listing days** – no insertion fees will apply.

- **1p gallery days** – the fee for gallery option is reduced.

- **5p listing days** – the insertion fee is reduced.

> **TIP** Take advantage of free listing days that occur on a Thursday. List on a ten day auction option which will end on a Sunday and incorporate the intermediate weekend.

Paying your fees

It is also worth mentioning at this time that as soon as you submit your auction, the listing fee will be charged to your account, along with any picture or upgrade fees. The final value fee will be calculated and charged at the end of the auction and debited from your selected payment method, either your bank account or credit card.

Summary

You should now:

- know what **eBay** is;

- know what **equipment** (computer, internet connection, camera, software) you need;

- have an idea of **what sells on eBay** (and what doesn't sell);

- know how to **research** the market (for items and eBay users);

- have established your **eBay account**;

- know **who you are going to be selling to**, and where they are in the world;

- have established your Terms & Conditions of trading;

- have decided on what **types of payment** to accept; and

- understand **eBay's fee structure**.

You're now ready to start preparing for the first auction. On to the next chapter!

Preparing for the first auction

Overview
Check the competition
Prepare your item
Packaging materials
Post
Photographs

Overview

The first auction can be a little daunting. There are new skills to learn and a new process to follow to complete your first eBay listing. The key element before this takes place is to prepare, so that when you are presented with a question during the process, you already have an idea of how you want to proceed.

Selling is basically a case of supply and demand: the more identical items that are for sale at any one time, the lower the price falls. If the item is rare or unusual, or maybe the only one of its kind for sale, then the price is likely to rise.

This chapter will tackle the research that is required to ensure that you sell the right item at the right time. Using the eBay systems and search engines, it is possible to predict how successful your item will be in the current market and indicate how it may be possible to present it in a slightly different way to maximise the final sale price.

Before offering an item for sale, it is important to have an idea about what will happen when the auction ends. The size and weight of your package may well affect the delivery time to the buyer and considerations like this will alter the design of the auction. We will work through the process in this chapter in reverse order – by understanding how we will pack and send the item, completing the auction will be that much easier.

Check the competition

This is the time for specific research into the track record of the item you are intending to sell. The rule of supply and demand will apply: if the supply is greater than the demand, then prices will not reach a high level. If on the other hand you have an item that is in high demand, and rare on eBay, it will do well.

Use the search facility

Now that you have selected the item you wish to sell, you can use the search facility to see how many other similar items are currently listed, and by using the advanced search and ticking 'completed listings' you will be able to see an indication of the prices your item is fetching.

- If you have an item that is **not common** on eBay, then you may not be able to gather any information from the search.

- If, on the other hand, you are going to sell a **very common** item, then the item may only reach a low price, or may not sell at all.

Using the search facility before you start will save a lot of work if the item is not in demand and may not sell. It is always better to spend your time selling something that has demand, rather than just shifting items for a few pence.

What has recently sold and for how much

While you are checking out the competition to see how your item may perform, make some notes about the auctions you visit. There is always a lot to be gained by seeing how other sellers present their items. Here are a few ideas:

- **Keywords in the title**
  If other sellers are selling the same item, they are very likely to be using the best key search words. Make a note of any that you think could be of use.

- **Starting price**
  Check the starting prices of the auctions; are they lower or higher than the price you were thinking of starting at?

- **Reserve price**

  Are the other sellers using a reserve price? If so, is this affecting the bidding?

- **Format of auctions**

  Are the auctions running in a standard format or are there any fixed price listings? This may give you an idea of the best format to use.

- **Competitor postage charges**

  Compare the postage charges that other sellers are applying. If they are much more than you were intending to charge, maybe the fact that you offer cheaper postage could be placed into the title as well. Maybe you could offer your item with postage at cost.

TIP If you find that several sellers have a different postage charge than you, re-weigh your item, just to make sure you are correct.

- **Do other sellers post overseas?**

  Check to see if there is a relationship between the price an item has reached and the market that the sellers sell into. The larger the market (i.e. if you sell worldwide), the higher the price should be. There are of course some items which just weigh too much and they are only ever likely to be sold within the UK.

- **How many hits have the auctions received?**

  If the sellers have opted to include a counter within their auctions, check how many hits they have had. Does the use of keywords in the title make an impact on the number of visits? This might help with the selection of the search words that will drive the most bidders to your auction.

Prepare your item

Before you sell any item, a little preparation will help the item sell and reach its best price. It may seem like common sense, but if you have already looked at some of the auctions, you will know that many sellers do not prepare their item for sale.

So, some recommendations follow for preparing your item to sell:

1. **Clean it**

   Take the time to ensure your item looks its best in the picture. If it has been stored, brush off the dust and remove any marks that can be seen. Close-up pictures show every aspect of the item, including any blemishes.

2. **Mend it**

   When selling items that are damaged or need replacement parts, repair these if you can. For example, just changing the hub caps on a car will improve the overall look and the first impression.

3. **Present it**

   Stage your pictures. Try to suggest how the item could be used, be creative. If selling furniture for a doll house, prepare a room setting rather than just laying out the items for the picture. Take close-up pictures of any key pieces. If you sell clothes, fold them neatly and arrange them in the picture, use hangers if they help or even invest in a tailor's dummy.

Packaging materials

The packaging of your item is one of the things that you will be judged on as a seller – how the item arrives at the buyer's address will determine the kind of feedback you receive. Broken items, or scratched paintwork, will not make the buyer feel as though they have traded with somebody who really cares. They may not return to your site again and may also mention the packing quality in their feedback.

Send items in such a way that you would be pleased to see them arrive at your door. Even if the item sold for only a small amount, send it on its way with care; you may see the buyer return for a larger purchase.

There are so many different types of item that can be sold on eBay, and most of them will need to be packed before they can be posted. The huge variety of goods for sale means that it's difficult to be specific here about individual items, but there are some general points to bear in mind when thinking about sending your item.

What you will need

There is a vast amount of packaging materials available. These can be purchased from retail shops or from eBay itself. When starting to sell, recycle anything you can and visit your local store to see if they are disposing of anything that could be of use.

Bubble wrap

The best invention ever made for an eBay seller! It is light, strong and not too expensive. The size of the bubbles does vary, so if you are going to order without seeing the actual wrap, make sure you get the correct size for your items.

 TIP Order your bubble wrap through eBay. As you can see in the screen shot overleaf, there's plenty of competition in this market and you will often get a special deal.

Fig 7. Search for bubble wrap

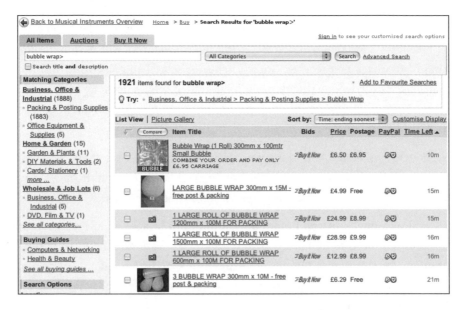

Boxes

Buying your boxes a few at a time can be very expensive, but if you know that the items you sell are the same size, you should be able to work out the best box size. They will be sent flat, so you will have to assemble them before they can be packed. Boxes can of course also be purchased through eBay in a variety of shapes and sizes. When I last looked there were 509 active auctions selling cardboard boxes.

Below is an example of what you are likely to pay for 25 of the most popular box sizes.

- Size 127 x 127 x 127mm – £11.00

- Size 203 x 152 x 102mm – £14.00

- Size 305 x 229 x 127mm – £18.50

- Size 279 x 254 x 115mm – £19.00

- Size 432 x 254 x 153mm – £22.00

TIP When sending boxes overseas, cut off some of the flaps to save on weight and therefore cost. The box will remain strong enough.

Bubble bags

Bubble bags also come in an assortment of sizes and the bigger they are, the more they cost. Use the smallest bags you can for the type of item and buy in bulk as well.

Buying just one bag from the Post Office or a similar retail shop will be very expensive. Check local wholesalers in your area and buy in quantities of at least 100 to get the price of each bag down to a reasonable level. Here is an example of what you are likely to pay for 100 of the most popular bag sizes, along with an idea of what will fit in them.

- Size A (110 x 160mm) jewellery, watches – £4.70

- Size B (120 x 210mm) floppy discs – £6.00

- Size C (150 x 210mm) CDs – £6.00

- Size D (180 x 260mm) A5 size DVDs/videos – £7.50

- Size E (220 x 260mm) small giftware – £10.00

- Size F (220 x 330mm) small books, software – £14.00

- Size G (240 x 330mm) A4 size brochures, literature – £14.00

- Size H (270 x 360mm) larger books – £20.00

- Size J (300 x 440mm) small clothing – £26.00

- Size K (350 x 470mm) A3 size – £29.00

Prices exclude vat and shipping.

TIP Check out some of the high street discount shops as they often have reasonably priced bubble bags.

Parcel wrapping paper

To add that extra security to your parcels, consider using brown paper to wrap them in. This can be purchased on large rolls and does add a professional touch at the same time. A large roll of paper may well work out to be too heavy to buy on the internet; the delivery charges will be very high. Instead, check your local phone book for suppliers in your area and buy several rolls in one visit.

Tape

Sticky tape will be used on almost every item: parcel tape for the actual package, clear tape to hold things together while you pack them, and maybe also 'fragile' tape.

Where to source the materials

- **When starting out**
  Don't throw anything away: recycle boxes and bubble bags from any items you buy, and obtain bubble wrap from the grocery department at your local supermarket.

- **Retail outlets**
  Check your local high street discount stores. Reduce costs where possible: cheaper tape might be a good idea, but keep some good quality tape for parcels to be sent by surface mail, as it will need to hold together for up to 8 weeks.

- **eBay sellers**
  There are many sellers of packing materials on eBay. They sell to other sellers and will have what you need. There will be a delivery overhead. However, with a little planning, you will be able to order in bulk. (And, of course, you will collect another feedback rating for trading with them.)

 TIP Invest in an electric paper shredder (you can buy one from Argos for about £20). Shredded paper makes great packing material and you will finally have a use for all the unsolicited mail that comes through your letterbox.

Storage

Storing your packing materials can be a problem and you should give some thought to this before you order in any quantity. It could be a safety hazard as these materials are combustible, but you also need to have them to hand when you are packing to save as much time as possible.

That special touch

How your buyer receives their item may well determine if they will visit you again. They will expect what they purchased to be delivered in a timely manner, but will also expect the packaging to be of a certain standard. Getting this final aspect correct will make all the difference.

Take that little bit of extra care when packing and turn this into one of your key selling points, 'trade with us and we promise top quality packaging'. This may just place you one step ahead of the competition and it need not cost much more to achieve.

Include a note of thanks

It is always a nice touch to include a note with the item thanking the buyer for their business, and it can easily br printed from your computer. Why not take it a little further and ask the bidder to visit again for more great items. Reassure them that should anything not be as they had expected with the item that you will put things right. Occasionally things do go wrong and it is much better for the buyer to contact you first, rather than leave negative feedback, so include this on your note.

Addressing

Ensure the package is addressed correctly

On the front of the package, write clearly, or print the delivery address, using all of the address including the postcode. Give the parcel every chance of arriving at the correct address.

TIP When sending heavy items, write the weight on the front, the Post Office will thank you for this.

Include a return address label

Having a return address is a good idea for anything sent through the mail. Not many items get lost, but if they do, there is always the chance the package can be sent back to you.

TIP Writing out the return address on each parcel can become a bit tedious, so consider having some labels printed; they are very reasonably priced and many companies offer the service. If having them printed, include the word 'from' or 'sender' and at the end of the address add 'UK', then when sending overseas, you won't have to keep adding the extra words. Visit www.able-labels.co.uk for an idea of prices. 1,000 labels will cost you about £5.

Five tips for top class packaging

1. **Over-protect your items**

   Damaged items cause bad feeling, they can cost time and money to put right and could result in bad feedback. Pack everything well first time.

2. **Establish a stock of packing materials**

   You cannot afford to run out of packing materials, and it takes too much time to search for the correct box. Make sure there are enough boxes or bags available.

3. **Recycle anything that can be re-used**

   Particularly in the early days, re-use anything that you have. It will save money and it is good for the environment.

4. **Decide how to pack the item before you sell it**

   Plan ahead with your packaging and you will be able to pack and send the item much quicker when the auction ends. You will also be able to get a better postage estimate for the auction.

5. **Preparation area**

   Having a dedicated area for packing is ideal; it saves time getting all the materials out and then packing them away again. If this is not possible, do your packing in one session, it will save time.

One of my lost parcels returned from the Netherlands after seven weeks, and I have recently had a fancy dress costume returned from the Czech Republic, so return labels have worked for me.

Post

The postage charges are a major element of your overall cost. The higher the postage charge, the higher the overall cost to the bidder. This may well restrict the price that your item reaches. Bidders like to know the postage charges, as this will allow them to appreciate the full cost of the item before they bid.

For smaller items, use a set of digital scales as mistakes can be very expensive. It costs about one penny per gram to send something to the US by Royal Mail airmail, so it is easy to lose profit by guessing what the postage costs will be.

This section concerns postage, both the charges and the companies that offer delivery services that can be used by eBay sellers. I will outline the services from the Royal Mail as these are likely to be the most commonly used, but also discuss some of the specialised carriers as well.

Carriers

Royal Mail

For most items, you are likely to use the Post Office, so visit their website at **www.royalmail.com** and print off the postage rates for both first and second class mail into the UK, and the airmail and surface mail rates. At the time of writing, the prices overleaf were the effective rates:

Table 10: Royal Mail UK charges

Service	Cost
First Class	Prices start at just 32p and most parcels are delivered the next working day.
Second Class	Prices start from 23p and most parcels are still delivered the next working day.
Recorded Signed For	A cost of 66p plus your First or Second Class postage. Provides automatic receipt and signature on arrival.
Standard Parcels	Send parcels up to a weight of 20 kilos with prices starting at £3.85. Delivery is within three to five working days.
Business collections	All your business mail collected from your work place and the service is free if you spend over £15,000 a year on Royal Mail services. It is possible to save money when you share the same collection point with other businesses.

International postage services are also available from the Royal Mail, and there are a number to choose from.

Table 11: Royal Mail international charges

Service	Cost
Airmail	Parcels can be sent virtually anywhere in the world with prices starting from 44p. Most mail is delivered within three to five days, depending on destination.
Surface mail	About half the price of airmail, this method is ideal for larger parcels. Delivery to Western Europe can be up to two weeks, up to five weeks for Eastern Europe, and up to twelve weeks for the rest of the world.
Airsure	Fast, secure and reliable airmail with electronic tracking to 28 destinations. Parcels will receive priority handling in the UK and abroad.
International Signed for	A signature is taken at the point of delivery. This service is available to almost every country and costs from £3.50 plus the airmail postage.

Specialised carriers

For larger parcels and for special deliveries, you may choose to use the services of a specialised carrier. They each have a range of delivery options, so you should be able to find the best service to suit your requirements. A few of the main carriers are listed in the table below.

Table 12: Specialised carriers

Carrier	Services offered
Parcel Force Worldwide www.parcelforce.com	Delivery across the UK, with next working day delivery to most locations by 9am, plus online ordering and collection. Delivery to all European countries, with next working day delivery to most major cities. Delivery to 240 destinations, from 2 working days, plus other less urgent services.
Delivery Networks www.deliverynetworks.co.uk Delivery Networks act as an agent for major parcel carriers. Just submit your requirements and you will receive a quote directly from the carrier.	A range of same day services for parcels or documents that need to be sent urgently within the UK. A range of worldwide road and air services. International services offered are guaranteed, can be tracked and offer insurance options. Account facilities with leading carriers if your volume of packages is greater than five a day. For smaller volumes, use their 'Send a Parcel', which again can be tracked and has insurance options.

Carrier	Services offered
DHL in partnership with 'Parcel to go' www.parcel2go.com This site offers reduced rates to eBay members with prices starting at £8.99. It also provides packaging advice and the ability to print your own customs documents.	Next day delivery into the UK. Guaranteed delivery options into the UK before 10am and before 5.30pm. International services.
TNT www.tnt.com TNT have a distribution network within the UK and international operations focused in Europe, Asia, North and South America.	An online price calculator which provides a guide price for your shipment. Online collection booking services. The ability to track your parcel via six different methods. Freephone collection booking service.

Each of the above companies will offer very similar services; some will provide incentives to eBay members and offer promotions from time to time. Do some research and decide which carrier best suits your needs, and, of course, check out the eBay discussion forums for real time comments from other users.

For the rest of this section I will concentrate on the standard Royal Mail rates as they will be used most frequently.

Other postal factors

TIP It is possible to notify the high bidder of the postage charges after the auction has ended. Do not do this. Work out the postage charges in advance, this will cut down on emails and result in more bids.

All of my items are currently sent via the Royal Mail. They are not particularly heavy, weighing no more than two kilos each. The basic postage services I use are:

- Second Class post: for items up to 1 kilo.

- First Class post: up to 1.25 kilos.

- Standard parcel post: up to 20 kilos.

- Airmail into Europe: up to 2 kilos.

- Airmail to the rest of the world: up to 2 kilos.

- Surface mail to the rest of the world: up to 2 kilos.

These are the services that I use to cover the majority of transactions, but they are not the only services available. It is possible to send items over 1 kilo by first class post, but this is more expensive and the point of the exercise is to make the postage costs as low as possible.

TIP It is worth mentioning that applying excessive postage costs are not a good idea. eBay frown on this, and your buyers may well reflect their disapproval in the feedback they leave – they will, of course, see the amount of postage you actually paid when they receive the item. It is fair to add costs for wrapping and packing materials, and even the cost of labour, but keep it to a reasonable level.

Delivery methods

Before you can calculate the postal costs, you will need to decide where in the world you are prepared to send the item and how many alternatives you will offer. As a general rule, offer First and Second Class rates in the UK and for overseas postage quote airmail into Europe and worldwide. This will be three or four postage rates that need to be calculated and added into the auction. If bidders require any other options, they will email you and ask.

Exploit postal rate bands

Postage rates are currently in fixed bands based upon the weight and dimensions of the item. You may find that with certain items you may be able to adjust the quantity a little, or pack it in a different way, and find that the postage drops into a lower band. If the item is 'fluid', such as coins, Lego or even multiple CDs, the removal of a few items may drop the postage to the next level, making the overall cost more attractive. This will not work with all types of item, of course, but it may make you a little more competitive.

It may be possible to send the item in more than one package. This may save on postage, and might also open up the overseas market. If your item is just over 2 kilos, for example, by dropping the weight of the main package under this level and then sending a second, smaller packet, international members may decide to bid.

How will the item be packaged?

Before you can weigh and measure the item and calculate the postage costs, you will need to give some thought to the packaging materials to be used as these will add to the overall weight. Small items such as CDs, DVDs, videos, batteries, etc will fit into a bubble bag and the weight of this packing can be taken into account. For larger items, make an allowance for a box or wrapping and remember to add it to the weight of the item when calculating the cost.

Estimated time for delivery

If an item is too heavy for normal post, it may be worth noting in the auction as it will take longer to arrive; or you could offer the buyer the option to pay for a premium delivery service.

I have found that within the UK, both First and Second Class parcels normally arrive the next working day, while standard parcel post takes up to 5 days. Airmail takes between 4 and 6 days, and surface mail can be anything up to 8 weeks. These delivery times will get longer in the run up to Christmas as you would expect.

Five top tips for postage

1. **Keep the postage costs as low as possible**
   Don't leave yourself open to bad feedback by overcharging for the postage. Work out a reasonable figure based on your full costs.

2. **Offer more than one option for the UK**
   Give your customers the choice. They may not be in a hurry and opt for the cheaper rate, or they may need it the next day and be prepared to pay for the service.

3. **State international postage options in the auction**
   If selling overseas, state the appropriate shipping charges – it will save time replying to emails. Help the bidder work out the true cost and update the automatic invoice with the relevant costs.

4. **Don't underestimate the weight of packaging**
   Things are always heavier than they look! Underestimating the weight of an item which sells outside of the UK will cost you money.

5. **Maximise the postage cost bands**
   Get to know the postal bands and adjust your auctions where appropriate so that the item, when packed, is within the cheaper banding.

Photographs

A picture is worth a thousand words

In the early days of eBay, and even as recently as just two years ago, many auctions did not have any pictures,. Now almost every auction will have at least one picture and it seems crazy that auctions could be listed without a picture.

Taking a great picture of your item is one of the most important elements of a successful sale on eBay, but it can also be a confusing area with several things to consider.

Taking pictures of your items will not only help to sell them more than anything else, but they will also save you a lot of time when it comes to the description. A well taken picture will say much more than you could write about the item and it is a lot quicker.

A close up picture of the reverse of a DVD or video, for example, removes the need to re-write the description or track listing; this saves time and shows the condition of the item both back and front.

This section covers what type of camera to use, choosing your background, lighting the photography area and preparing your item for sale.

Camera types

Choosing the right camera for the job can be confusing as there are hundreds now available. This section looks at some of the basic requirements that you should look for.

Film v digital

It is possible to convert photographs taken with a film camera to digital format (which is needed for eBay), but the process incurs unnecessary cost and time. Possibly a case for still using a film camera could be made for very inactive sellers of high priced items, but the case wouldn't be made on quality grounds – even a cheap digital camera produces images easily good enough for display on eBay auction pages.

So, an active eBay seller needs a digital camera. The cost of digital cameras is now so low that not buying one is a false economy.

When purchasing your digital camera, look for one that will be easy to use – the more facilities it has, the longer it will take to master them. (Remember how long it took you to master your video recorder!) Check that the documentation is easy to understand and choose a camera that matches your own experience. If digital photography is new to you, choose a 'point and click' model to start with.

Camera specifications

The great thing about eBay is that it does not require you to have the most up to date camera with many millions of pixels. In fact, if the picture quality is too good, they may not even load onto the system.

The following is a list of camera functions which I have found to be ideal for eBay:

Close-up

The close-up function will allow you to take high quality pictures of subjects very close to the lens. These work very well with small items, or for photographing words or instructions.

> As the majority of items I sell are relatively small, I tend to use the close-up function all of the time.

Rear view screen

The rear view screen will show the actual picture that will be taken. Just position the item within the screen and the picture will be exactly as you see it.

> I have used four different cameras over the years and have settled on a FujiFilm FinePix A203 model, which has a rear view window. Now I just stage the picture, check through the rear view screen and click.

Flash

The flash function of a camera will produce enough artificial light to take pictures. Although it does tend to alter the colour of some items and can produce strange effects where the light bounces back from a shiny surface.

> After many trials using the flash function, I have decided to improve my natural light sources as much as possible, which I feel makes a better picture. Experiment with your camera and settle on a method that works for you.

Pixel number

Pixels are the small dots that make up a digital picture. Your television screen is constructed in much the same way: the more pixels in a picture, the greater the quality of the image.

Cameras are sold quoting the maximum number of pixels that pictures can have. These limits are increasing all of the time, but more pixels means larger file sizes to store them. So, the higher the quality of the picture, the fewer pictures can be taken and stored on the camera at one time. As the number of pixels decreases, you can take more pictures before you have to transfer them to your computer.

Pictures that are hosted by eBay are reduced in size to fit with the standard templates, so the original size will not really be an issue.

> I currently use a 2 million pixel camera, which, today, is quite modest, but this quality level is more than adequate for eBay.

USB connection

Older cameras used to connect with the computer through a serial port. This is a slow type of connection that often requires rebooting the computer when attaching the camera. Ensure your camera has a USB connection. This will transfer your pictures faster and is easier to set up.

Memory size

Many digital cameras are sold with a very small memory capacity (e.g. 16MB). This is too small to store many photographs on. When buying a camera it is a good idea to buy a larger memory disc at the same time – 64MB or higher is recommended.

To give an idea of memory card prices and an idea of the sizes available, below are a few examples from www.picstop.co.uk. I have shown the options for a FujiFilm camera, although similar cards for other makes will cost much the same. For the sake of comparison, I have also added the current purchase prices that were available from eBay on the same day.

- Fuji 64MB xD Picture Card – £9.90 (eBay £9.24 inc postage)

- Fuji 128MB xD Picture Card – £11.60 (eBay £11.45 inc postage)

- Fuji 256MB xD Picture Card – £21.10 (eBay £16.60 inc postage)

- Fuji 512MB xD Picture Card – £35.40 (eBay £29.62 inc postage)

Postage for one card – £1.90, subsequent cards 40p each, prices include VAT.

A good explanation of camera memory can be found at: www.pcphotoreview.com/memoryguidecrx.aspx

Background for the picture

As you browse through eBay, look at the backgrounds that sellers use for their pictures. Some are great, and some, such as highly patterned carpets, don't work at all.

To display your item well choose a backdrop that is clean, bright and not cluttered. Avoid strong patterns on table tops, curtains and so on. Instead, make up a temporary studio in a well lit area. Drape a sheet over some boxes and experiment with different colours until you find something that works well and is convenient.

The quality of your pictures will help sell your item; make a good job and take the trouble to prepare your photography area.

Lighting

Natural light is the best to use when taking pictures, however this can prove very tricky during the winter months. Many sellers use light boxes or similar studio systems – these will allow you to take pictures at any time and can be purchased on eBay and at photography shops.

Try not to take pictures under artificial light as they do appear very dark and often change the colour of the item. Some cameras have a setting for artificial light, which might be a solution to the problem.

> I still use natural light and take as many pictures as I can on well lit days and store these on my computer. Ensuring a well stocked library of pictures means that I can list items when I wish to.

As a general rule, make your photography area as well lit as you can and reduce shadows.

Saving pictures on your PC

Folders

Within your computer, create a dedicated folder in which you can store your eBay pictures. This will again save time at a later stage. It might be worth splitting this folder into different sub-folders for each month, so that all of the pictures for items sold during, say, August appear in the same place on your computer. The same procedure can be used for different types of items, maybe a separate folder for DVDs, computer games or shoes. If you sell seasonal items, separate folders for the time of year might work well.

File names

When saving pictures on to your computer, select a name for the picture that relates to the actual item; this will make it much easier to find again. Your camera software will allocate a unique number to each picture, which will just be a numerical reference. By changing the picture name, you will save time when searching for it during the listing process.

For example, if you are selling a pair of brown shoes, it might be an idea to take three pictures; one from each side and a picture of the soles. Naming your pictures could be something like:

- Picture 1: brownshoes-left.jpg

- Picture 2: brownshoes-right.jpg

- Picture 3: brownshoes-sole.jpg

This name format will ensure that the three pictures are grouped together in your picture folder, making them easier to find and load.

In a later section I will discuss how to load your pictures directly into the auction, bypassing the eBay system – there are considerable cost savings to be made by doing this. By using the naming convention above, the later section will become much easier.

Format

I will discuss the various formats of files, and pictures in particular, in a later section, however, for now, if you save your pictures in a JPG format, you will not have any problems with eBay.

What is a JPG file?

The JPG file extension (pronounced 'Jay Peg') is the correct format for photo images that are intended to be used on websites or for email. The JPG file is compressed by 90%, or to only 1/10 of the size of the original data, which is very good for transferring between computers (i.e. loading pictures onto eBay).

However, this compression efficiency comes with a price. JPG files will lose some image quality when the JPG data is compressed and saved, and this quality can never be recovered. You can show a JPG file smaller than the original size, but if you try and enlarge it, it will be poor quality.

Editing your pictures

Almost all digital cameras come with software that allows you to download the pictures to your computer. Often this software also allows you to edit and make simple corrections, such as adjusting the size of your pictures. Failing this, you should be able to use a standard photo editor program to alter your pictures.

Photo editing programs

There are some great photo editing programs available on the internet, and many of them are free. The free software packages that are available may have some restrictions, they may be older versions of the program or may not have as many features as the current release. The company offering the free software will, of course, try to convince you to buy the most up to date edition.

Check some of these free websites, there may be just the one you are looking for.

Table 13: Photo editing programs

Program	Description
Serif PhotoPlus 6 www.freeserifsoftware.com	Serif gives away previous versions of their software to entice users to purchase the current version. At the time of printing, you could still download a completely free version of PhotoPlus 6. PhotoPlus 6 is an image editing software that allows you to create, manipulate, and enhance photographs, bitmap graphics, and web animations, just about everything you would ever need for your eBay pictures. All the tools you need are provided in the download, along with handy hints for some great results.
GIMP www.gimp.org	GIMP is a popular image editor with many of the features of higher priced programs. It is a freely distributed piece of software for such tasks as photo retouching, image composition and image authoring. It works on many operating systems, in many languages. There may be some issues surrounding the frequency of software updates, although it does work well with Windows.

Program	Description
Ultimate Paint www.ultimatepaint.com	Ultimate Paint is great for image creation, viewing, and manipulation. It was designed to be fast and compact. It can be used to retouch and enhance photos and has a set of built-in tools. Features include resizing, rotating, flood filling and text operations. It is ideal for both novice users and experts alike.
Pixia park18.wakwak.com/~pixia/	Pixia was originally developed in Japan and is now available in an English version. It is a free painting and retouching software, featuring custom brush tips, multiple layers, masking, vector- and bitmap-based drawing tools, colour, tone, and lighting adjustments and multiple undo/redo.
ImageForge www.cursorarts.com	ImageForge is a freeware image editor with painting and editing tools. With this program you can import images from scanners and digital cameras. Some of the tools will allow you to apply special effects filters, and create photo albums and slideshows. This software program is very similar to Microsoft Paint, with a few more options.

If you're using Microsoft, then the Paint program that comes bundled with Windows may be sufficient for many. This is what I use. It's usually nestled away under Programs > Accessories.

Orientation

While we are talking about editing pictures on the computer, an important thing to be able to do is to rotate your picture so that it always looks as it should. There is nothing worse than trying to look at a picture which has not been rotated and is still on its side. This happens quite often. If the item should be seen in an upright position, rotate the picture until it looks correct.

Five top tips for great pictures

1. **Keep it simple**
   Don't confuse the bidder with a complex picture: centre the item and focus the shot, ensuring that there are not any other items within the picture area. Don't get too artistic!

2. **Have a clean background**
   Choose your backdrop carefully. Erect a temporary studio if possible and ensure that the picture background presents the best image of your item.

3. **Use the best lighting available**
   Avoid shadows at all costs, dark pictures do not help sell items. Consider a lighting studio or light box.

4. **Rotate portrait pictures**
   There is nothing worse than having to twist your head round to see an item which has been photographed using a landscape picture, but has not been rotated. Turn your pictures so they look as they should.

5. **Be aware of the item scale**
   Include a scale reference within the picture, maybe a coin or ruler, just to ensure that the bidder understands how big the item is. (Especially true for rock groups buying models of Stonehenge!)

How many pictures?

Just how many pictures you decide to include in your auction will depend upon the item you are selling, how you want the overall presentation of the auction to look and any associated costs of adding extra pictures. In a later section, I will show you how to add extra pictures for no additional cost.

> I have settled on a three-picture format for the majority of my items. This includes the main shot which shows the whole item, and then two close-up pictures to show the finer detail. The most pictures I have ever used is 34 when I recently sold a car. This auction also allowed the visitor to hear the engine running by downloading a small sound file. This unusual approach to the auction resulted in three times as many hits as similar cars were receiving.

References

Digital photography is a huge topic, that would need a whole book to itself to properly explain. So treat the above as just an overview, with the most important points highlighted. If you're completely new to digital cameras, then the references below should help.

www.vividlight.com/articles/3016.htm – Quite a detailed explanation of digital photography.

www.betterphoto.com/article.asp?id=39 – How to take photos for eBay

www.pcworld.com/howto/article/0,aid,112658,00.asp – ditto

www.imaging-resource.com – A good reference for selecting a digital camera (check out 'Dave's Picks')

Summary

You should now have:

1. checked the **competition;**

2. **prepared** your item;

3. got your **packaging materials** ready;

4. worked out the **post** methods and costs; and

5. **photographed** the item and have the photo files stored on your computer.

You should now be ready to create your first auction!

But, just before moving on to that, I list briefly below some things to think about before all your auctions.

Five top tips before the auction

1. **Check the competition regularly**
   Trends on eBay are always changing, so make sure that you have the right items for sale at the right time.

2. **Check completed auctions**
   Use the completed auction search to find out how prices are holding up for other auctions on eBay. You should be able to work out a trend: if they are falling fast, consider a shorter auction duration or holding onto the stock until prices pick up.

3. **Be open to new ideas**
   Consider any new ideas that you might come across, evolve wherever you can, keep one step ahead of the competition.

4. **Compare postage costs against your own**
   High postage costs really annoy buyers and if it is much higher than other auctions, it will deter bidders. Always compare with other sellers and keep them as low as possible.

5. **Research each new type of auction you run**
   If you start to sell a new type of item, check the whole eBay site and see how other sellers are listing, compare key search words and adapt to your own style.

Creating the first auction

Overview

The time has come to place your first auction on eBay. As with all things, it is easy when you know how!

This chapter provides a step by step guide to making that first leap into your online business. It contains the information you will be asked to submit, along with suggestions, hints, tips and 13,000 auctions' worth of experience which will drive your sale price higher.

The process to do this has recently changed,and this chapter will describe how to use the new 'Sell your item' form. The original process is still in use, so you may come across it. All the information is only the same, the order in which it is entered has altered.

The actual process is now completed in four stages:

1. Category selection

2. Create your listing

3. Promote and review your listing

4. Review your listing

eBay will guide you though each stage and if you've prepared well the actual process will be fine. The good news is that after you have completed one listing, the option exists to 'sell a similar item', so all of your terms and conditions, postage details and so on are retained, and you will not need to enter them again.

Stage 1: Category selection

The very first step in the selling process on eBay is to access the 'sell your item' form. This is done by clicking on the 'Sell' link which is on the top menu next to the 'Buy' link. If you are not already signed in, you will be asked to do so. When this screen has loaded, the process of category selection can begin.

Selection of category

There are hundreds of categories within the eBay system, and they are continually changing as products become fashionable or as trends end. In order to place your item onto the system, you must decide where best to put it.

The categories work on a 'menu/sub-menu' basis, just click the 'Browse for categories' link and the main categories will be shown. The first choice is to select the main category, perhaps 'Baby', then to pick the subcategory that best suits your item, perhaps 'baby feeding', and so on until there are no more options available and you see the message 'You have finished selecting a category. Click the Save and Continue button below.' If the subcategory has further options, it will have an arrow next to it and a new menu will appear.

eBay offers some help here. There is a category search engine which will suggest the most appropriate category; just type a keyword or phrase into the box on this page, maybe 'baby feeding', and the suggested categories will be shown. You can also see the last ten categories you listed in, which might help with the selection.

Check on other similar listings

Another great way of selecting the best category for your item is to see what the competition are doing. Type your item into the main search engine and all similar items will be found; by viewing them, you will be able to see where other sellers have placed their items.

Multiple categories

It is possible to list your item in more than one category. eBay currently make a charge for this, but it can increase the number of potential bidders that visit your auction. Approximately 25% of all sales are made to bidders who browse the categories for items, so for certain items a second category could prove very worthwhile. To add your item to a second category, just click 'Add a second category' and repeat the process.

TIP As a general rule when using the category selector, choose the category with the highest number of references to your item as this is likely to receive most visits by bidders searching for your item.

Second categories should only be used where the item logically fits into more than one. This does, however, require some understanding of what the other categories are. This knowledge can be gained by more research, using the suggested category search engine or searching for the item yourself. For example, if you are selling a collection of Thomas the Tank Engine trains made by Brio, two categories may be an option. There is a category for Thomas The Tank Engine, which will contain all manner of items with this theme, and there is also a category for Brio, again with a vast array of items. By placing your item in both categories, your item may be found by both Thomas and Brio browsers.

No logical category?

If your item has no logical category or subcategory, then eBay do offer a final option. At the bottom of most subcategory lists is one beginning 'Other'; this is not the best place to list your auction, but if all else fails, this will work, although you may not get many browsers. Another place to list items that are not mainstream is in the main category called 'Everything else'. There are some great subjects here and it is well worth checking out.

Once you have settled on a category for your item, just click 'Save and continue'.

Stage 2: Create your listing

The second section of the 'sell your item' form is known as 'Create Your Listing'. This section contains the title and description of your auction, pricing information and payment details.

This is the most important part of your auction, it is where you can describe the good and maybe bad points with the intention of making your item irresistible to any bidders. What you write in this section will either help the item to sell or increase the value of the bids or it could deter the visitor from placing a bid at all. Some of the shortest descriptions seen to date include 'see picture', 'as shown' and 'box of toys'. The picture, as we will see later in this section is undoubtedly the best selling aid, but do not overlook the impact that an accurate, descriptive and personal narrative can create.

It is not enough to just take a picture and submit a listing on eBay. There are so many items for sale, that if you do attract a visitor to your site, you need to actively sell the item. The fewer negative aspects you have to mention, the better your description will be. Highlight all of the positive points and sell your item as though it was your most cherished possession.

During the earlier research phase, you decided how your auctions should look, the layout, colour scheme, font size and so on, it is within this section that we will test out those ideas and see how they look.

Title

The title of your auction should be considered as the door to your shop, it is important to have as many visitors as possible and the title will attract them. eBay have some rules about the title space: the main one is the length of the field, the available space will count down from 55 with each character you enter.

Fig 8. Title and subtitle fields

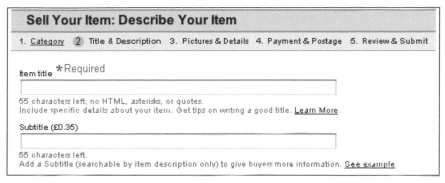

Add a subtitle (searchable by item description only) to give buyers more information.

TIP The title bar has 55 characters, use them all with as many key search words as you can fit in. The more information you can give your potential visitors, the more likely they are to click to see the auction.

Punctuation within the title space

The space within the title section is limited and as it forms the main entry point to your auctions it needs to have as many keywords in it as possible. It is therefore important not to repeat key search words.

For example, one of the most searched for words is 'toy', also searched for is the word 'toys', so on the face of it, a good title would have both of these words in it. eBay, however have altered the search engine for certain words and they return the same number of results. Search for 'toy' and then 'toys' and the number of results will be the same, allowing for any auctions that ended or began during the time it takes to complete the second search. Therefore do not waste space using both words.

This same principle also works with punctuation marks. The comma is ignored as is the slash and the full stop, along with several other characters, so you can punctuate your title without the fear of losing search results.

Keywords and phrases

75% of buyers search as opposed to browse for items. Therefore the trick is to get as many of the most searched for words into the title without keyword spamming. This is the annoying habit that some sellers employ to entice you into their auctions: they will include words within the title that do not relate directly to the item, but are popular search words. This practice is frowned upon.

> The top search words for each category are reproduced from time to time within eBay and by checking other similar auctions, you will be able to identify the keywords for your items. For example, the most searched for word or phrase is 'new', so if your item is in great shape, write 'as new' instead of 'great shape' and more potential buyers will find your item when they enter 'new'.

'In the style of'

Try and avoid using certain words which are used to place a key search word into the title. For example, if selling a mobile phone made by a less popular manufacturer, avoid words such as 'Nokia style', 'similar to Nokia', 'the same as Nokia' or 'not Nokia'. These words when used with any popular search word will drive more visits to your site, but the visitor will not have found the item they were looking for, in this case a Nokia phone. They are very likely to feel misled and are unlikely to buy. Instead try to build your auctions so that it contains elements of the branded item along with similar parts, making the title accurate. An example could include 'Nokia mobile phone case with charger & phone', here the case is made by Nokia. This is a more subtle way to use key search words.

Spelling

Check and double check the spelling of words in the title. If they are spelt incorrectly, then nobody will find them.

> Some of the classic spelling errors that I have made over the years include a great 'Simpsons Camra' instead of camera – that item didn't fetch very much, but did sell to a lover of real ale. I listed a super paperback by the author Terry Ratchett, which didn't get many hits and only received one bid. Even now I get it wrong – rushing the title section is not a good idea.

Subtitles

A subtitle on your auction can be used to provide bidders with more information and will also catch their eye as they browse down a list of search results.

Use the subtitle feature to:

- Highlight key selling points about your item (brand name, artist, designer, accessories or options).

- Provide additional information about the item that won't fit in the main title (item condition, benefits, specifications, model number, or any extras you might offer).

- Make your item stand out from other listings.

The subtitle contents are not included in the main search engine criteria, so ensure that all keywords are in the main title and supplementary information is in the subtitle.

Generally I do not use subtitles, they do of course eat into your profit as they currently carry an extra fee. But when selling a larger value item, such as a car, or more recently a collection of miniature Napoleonic lead models, they can work very well. In the case of the army of small soldiers, I sold them in 13 brigades, each with approximately 150 figures – it was quite an army! I used the subtitle to further describe the item and state which Brigade they were from.

Top tips for the title space

1. **Use all the space**

   Use as many of the 55 characters as you can, and make the title as comprehensive as possible.

2. **Ensure you use as many key search words as you can**

   Remember to use alternative keywords such as 'laptop' and 'notebook' when describing your item as bidders may search for both.

3. **Do not mislead your bidders**

   Don't get bidders to your auctions under false pretences by using keyword spamming. They won't thank you for it.

4. **Check your spelling**

   Keywords that are not spelt correctly will not work; double check your title before you submit the auction.

Pictures

As you have already written your description, now is the time to load onto eBay the picture you have taken and stored on your computer. This section of the form will allow you to load up to 12 pictures onto the system and the good news is that the first picture is free. There are two methods to enter pictures: you can use your own web hosting service and enter the URL (web address) of the picture (however this is not the most common option and does require a certain level of HTML knowledge), so for the rest of this section I will discuss the basic eBay Picture Service.

TIP Consider including a location map on a separate web page and include a hypertext link to it when selling items that can only be collected.

How to load the first picture

Fig 9. Picture upload screen

Reproduced with the permission of eBay Inc. COPYRIGHT © EBAY INC. ALL RIGHTS RESERVED

The first time you use the eBay Picture Service, you may be asked to download a small software program which allows this to take place. Then it is just a case of clicking the 'browse' button and finding the picture on your computer. This tends to be within the 'My Pictures' folder, although it could be on your desktop or any other location of your choosing. Just double click the picture or click once, select open and the address will be copied into the first picture box.

Don't use stock pictures

Try not to use stock or catalogue pictures, particularly if the item has been used. Bidders like to see the actual item they will receive. Representative pictures will reduce the number of bids you will receive, so avoid them.

Extra pictures

Extra pictures can be added using exactly the same process as you used for the first picture, although this time there is an additional fee for each extra picture.

Additional picture options

At this stage in the listing process, you will have a choice to select any picture options you wish to have in your auction. At the time of writing, there are three options and it is worth noting that the picture option selected will apply to all the pictures within the particular listing. Only your first picture within option one is free, the others carry additional fees which are detailed next to the selection boxes.

1. Picture Pack

Picture Pack is a discounted package deal of eBay Picture Services offerings.

You can:

- Add up to 12 pictures to your listing.
- Supersize all your pictures (up to 800 x 800 pixels).

- Use Picture Show to let buyers browse pictures or run them in a slide show at the top of the item page.

- Add Gallery to display a small image of your first picture when buyers search and browse.

2. Supersize pictures

Extra large pictures that are displayed within a 500 x 500 pixel area, or 800 x 800 pixel area if you have larger pictures. Visitors have the option to see your large pictures by clicking on a link.

Fig 10. Supersize pictures

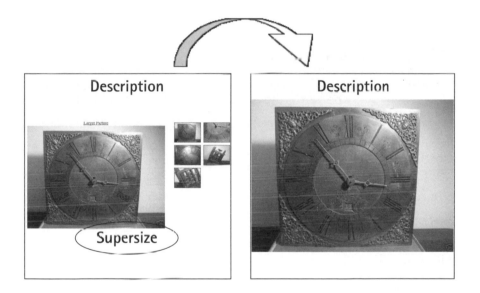

3.Picture Show

Your multiple pictures can be seen as a slideshow at the top of the auction page.

When you have selected the pictures you want, along with any additional picture options, click 'upload pictures'.

Gallery

You may already have seen gallery pictures when you were searching through eBay for research. They are the small pictures that are shown alongside your item title in the search results list. Items that do not have a gallery picture will show a small camera icon.

When to use the gallery option

The gallery option does carry an extra fee and you must decide if the value of your item warrants the extra expenditure. eBay inform us that using a gallery picture will increase the average final value by 12%, which means that any item selling for more than £2 should benefit from the gallery picture.

TIP Use extra pictures to show your item to its best. It's also useful if there is a lengthy description on the back of the item, perhaps a track listing on a CD or a summary of the contents. The time saved by not typing it out again may be worth the extra fee to load a second picture.

I use the gallery on the majority of my auctions. Whilst many listings on eBay still do not use it, I feel that the bidder's eye is drawn to items that have a small picture and they are tempted to look further. Once they have clicked through to the auction, it is then up to the seller to convince them to place a bid.

Additional item specifics

Most items on eBay can have some additional specifics added; these will vary from category to category. Options are many and varied, they include new/used, brand, colour, material, size, etc. Select the ones you want to include from the lists available. If it is a new item, ensure that you select this option as eBay operate a search option allowing buyers to find new items.

Description

Fig 11. Description page

Item description ✳

Describe your items features, benefits, and condition. Be sure to include in your description: Condition (new, used, etc.), original price, and dimensions or size. You may also want to include notable markings or signatures, or its background history. See more tips for <u>Business/ Management</u>.

Enter <p> to start a new paragraph. Get more <u>HTML tips</u>.

<u>Spell check</u> | <u>Preview description</u>

Note: After you click Continue, you may be asked to download a small file. This file will help you add pictures to your listing. If the next page does not appear, change your picture selection method.

The Item Description is the main space to sell your item to any potential bidders. It is essentially a blank page where you can enter anything you feel would increase the chance of a bid being made. A great description will include every detail so that the actual picture is not actually required – the bidder has enough information from the words alone (although always include the picture as well of course!)

There are two methods used to enter your auction description:

1. Standard.

2. HTML (the code that is used to create web pages).

Each of these methods has its advantages. The HTML section will be discussed in a later chapter, here we will continue with our auction using the standard method.

eBay formatting tools

In addition to a blank canvas, eBay have provided some basic tools which can enhance your description, making it easier to read, have more impact and ultimately to increase the amount of interest in the item. You will have seen from the research that you conducted earlier that many sellers do not use these tools, they will just type one continuous block of text, often in block capitals with no paragraphs. This is not easy to read and it is so easy to make a better job of the description.

The basic tools currently include:

- Font name.

- Size.

- Colour.

Each of these functions will help with the basic layout of the text in your description. Just select the way you would like it to appear, and try out a few different combinations until you settle on a format that you are happy with.

There are several other useful buttons here: just the same as with any word processor, you can make your text bold, underline it, place it in italics and justify it to the left, right or centre. You can also use the bullet functions to make the appearance of lists that much easier to read.

Perhaps one of the best tips I can give is to check the spelling before you move on. Descriptions that contain spelling mistakes may well suggest that little care has been taken with the listing, which is not the message we want to give.

The final tool within this section is called *inserts*. These can be used for some great additions to your listing and are covered in a later chapter in more detail. However, even at this stage you can click on the 'sellers other items' entry and eBay will create a direct link to your 'items for sale'

> As a general rule I have settled on Arial text with a size 12 font. I use black text for most of the description and red text for any titles or for important information.

page. You can then insert this into your listing where you want. The same works with the 'add to favourites list'; include this insert and if it is clicked on by a visitor, eBay will add your ID to their favourites list so they can visit you directly from their 'my eBay' page.

Don't worry about how this actually works; I will expand on some areas later, but you do not need to know the technology behind the facility.

Five top tips for the best description layout

1. **Use standard fonts**
   To ensure that all bidders see your description as you would wish, stick to standard fonts as some computers do not have a full range of fonts loaded.

2. **Keep it simple**
   Don't confuse your bidders with loads of detail that is not relevant to your auction; make your description easy to read and use colours to highlight key elements.

3. **Keep the layout as short as possible**
   Your bidders will lose interest if your description is too long and will leave to visit another auction. Do all you can to keep the listing as short as possible.

4. **DO NOT USE ALL CAPITALS**
   Descriptions with only capital letters are not professional. In the internet world, capitals are the equivalent of shouting. They are harsh and should be avoided. Use capitals sparingly to add emphasis to keywords or phrases.

5. **Restate the auction title**
   Remind the bidder what exactly is included in the auction by adding a title within the description.

Positive language

It is important to write the description of your item in such a way that it is accurate, and yet presented to ensure that any viewers of your auction appreciate all the good points. It is not a good idea to hide the truth, or not to mention any damage or defects, as you will annoy the buyer, may lose money on the trade and run the risk of receiving bad feedback.

However, there are some ways to cope with faults and damage. The words 'but' and 'however' are great for breaking up a descriptive line and have the effect of leaving the reader remembering the comments after the word. This can be used within the description, whilst still pointing out any damage. Rather than writing:

A great DVD, full of excitement and action, the case is broken.

Instead write:

A great DVD, the case is broken, but the film is full of excitement and action.

Always end on a positive note and be sure to list all of the good points.

Recently this has evolved, where something that would have been taken for granted at one time is now a positive selling point. For example, as there are so many imitations and copied DVDs in circulation, it is now useful to the bidder if you write 'this is not a copy or an import' and maybe mention the retail outlet where it was purchased. The bidder will have more confidence that they are bidding on the real item. By dealing with this issue in the listing, you will help the bidder make the decision to bid for your item.

Describing condition

It is important to describe the condition of your item. If it is new, then it is easy, but if the item has been used, then using words such as 'good' or 'fair' could lead to some confusion. Good condition will mean different things to different people. Try to stay away from subjective descriptions and be accurate. And remember that some people will place as much value on the box or label than the item itself.

Mention any faults with the item along with any positive aspects. With a CD, for example, rather than say that the condition is good, mention the scratches on the case, but also mention that the disc itself is not scratched. The words 'as new' can result in a lot of misunderstandings as some bidders might expect things to be near perfect, while others may consider it to be 'as new' taking into account the age of the item.

Use as many relevant words as possible

Searches made where the bidder clicks 'in titles and descriptions' will find all the keywords in the title space, but also any in the description. Therefore if you could not fit all the keywords into the title, enter them in this space and bidders will still find your listing. Experience will show exactly which words to include.

Do not just include words that have no relevance to the item to drive up the number of hits; this is keyword spamming – it annoys bidders and eBay take a very dim view of it.

TIP The use of abbreviations can cause some problems, especially if you are selling to a worldwide market – so try to avoid them. For example, the letters PAL used for a video system indicate that the video will only work in a certain area. However, just writing that it is a PAL format may not be enough, mention as well that not all players can take this format and that the bidder must check their system for compatibility.

Positive points

Enter as many positive points about the item as you can. Perhaps the clothing you are selling comes from a non-smoking home, or one with no pets. These things can make an impact on a bidder's decision, so let them know. If something has been used only once, maybe you played the game only once, this will provide the bidder with an idea of the condition.

Tell your bidder why it is for sale, but be careful not to 'shoot yourself in the foot'. Selling a computer game because 'it is just too hard for my son' will not encourage other parents to buy it for their son. Perhaps mention that you have an unwanted Christmas gift, or two of an item, maybe you finished the computer game and have moved on to the next one – let the bidders know.

Describe the actual item

Try not to use standard descriptions of your item, which can be obtained from the internet. A description in your own words will make the item seem more personal. Use technical descriptions if they are available, but include only the relevant points.

Using links to other pages that contain additional specifications for the item has both advantages and disadvantages. The good point is that you will not have to write such a long description, however the viewer may not click the link, or it may not work and they will move on to another auction.

TIP If providing measurements of your item, use both cm and inches. Some bidders still use imperial sizes and most of America understand feet and inches.

Make it personal

If you are selling your own items, describe how you used the item. Mention any special aspects of the item; if they are compatible with other similar makes, tell the bidder. If you are selling DVDs or CDs, describe the mood they create: 'ideal driving music', or 'just what you need for a lazy Sunday afternoon', and so on.

Benefits not features

Rather than describe the features of your item, tell your bidders what benefits they will see from the item, as this will help them to imagine it in their own home. For example, if you are selling a cot mobile for a baby's room, describe how the musical cot mobile allowed you to get baby to sleep quicker so that you could spend more time elsewhere, instead of just stating the songs it plays.

Mention other items for sale

One of the most successful additions to the description section is the ability to 'cross sell' and 'up-sell' your items. If a bidder has reached your site looking for a pair of walking boots, and you are also selling a walking stick, why not let them know. The bidder may end up bidding on both items or maybe just the second item, but the longer they spend looking at your items, the more likely they are to bid somewhere.

Potential bidders can check the other items that you have for sale from the menu towards the top of the screen, but this involves scrolling up the page and they do not know at that time that you have something else that may be of interest to them, so they may not check your other items without some prompting.

There are several ways to cross sell your items. The easiest is simply to mention in your description that you are also selling other items that may be of interest. Remember to mention them by name rather than:

Please check our other great items.

which may not entice them as much as:

If you are looking for walking boots, please check out our walking stick and jacket.

Use the insert 'sellers other items' as described above to give them a convenient link to your 'items for sale' page.

Included in a future chapter will be two more methods to cross sell your items, using direct hypertext links to the auctions and also using pictures as links. These picture links will show the viewer exactly what the item is and when clicked they will be taken to the auction directly.

After much experimentation, I now have two cross selling links in each of my auctions – they both contain pictures of the other auctions and hypertext 'live links' to them. Two links with a small description of each item will fit nicely onto one line of the page and they do not detract from the main auction. Experience has shown that promoting 'weaker' items in this way will increase the number of hits received and will result in higher prices.

In a similar way, if you have more of the item for sale in another auction, mention that in the description as well: 'This is just part of my collection of Smurfs listed at the moment, please check out my other auctions for more.'

> Buyers will always be on the lookout for a discount. I offer a reduction in postage for multiple purchases and by listing similar items over a number of days can entice the buyer back to my auctions many times.

Five top tips for the best content

1. **Be accurate**

   Include both good and bad points, don't run the risk of bad feedback. There are positive ways to describe faults in your item, practise with different techniques.

2. **Do not use abbreviations**

   Write your description in plain English. Abbreviations that are used in the UK may not be recognised overseas and it could lead to confusion.

3. **Sell the experience not just the item**

   Sell the whole experience of the item, not just the article itself. Help your bidder to imagine owning it and the pleasure it will give them.

4. **Cross sell your other auctions**

   Make reference to your other auctions. Use the description, hypertext links or even picture links, but make sure your bidders know about your other items.

5. **If possible, make the auction personal**

   Try to make your auction as personal as possible so that every visitor feels that you are speaking directly to them. Remember: people buy from people.

Listing designers

eBay have created a number of patterned borders known as 'listing designers' that place a themed edge around your description. There are several to choose from so you can match the best one to your item. You can select a listing designer at this stage and see how it looks when you preview your auction, you can then change it if you wish or remove it altogether before submitting your listing.

Alternative designs

eBay will make a charge for a listing designer, so you may wish to create your own border. In a later section, I will expand on this and demonstrate how it can be achieved with only a very basic understanding of HTML code.

Visitor counters

You can add a counter to your listing at this point, and there is a choice of styles. Counters will give you an idea of the number of visitors to your auction. This should help you judge if you have the correct title and search words.

The next section of the form details the way in which you are going to place your listing on eBay. With a title of 'How you're selling', it includes details of price and duration.

Selling format

This section gives you the option to sell your item at an:

1. online auction.

2. at a fixed price. Or

3. eBay Express, if applicable to your item.

There is a minimum number of feedbacks required before the fixed price option can be used, so it may not be available for the first few auctions.

Fixed price option

The fixed price option works exactly as you would expect. If you know how much you would like for the item, use this method and the bidders will be able to decide whether to purchase there and then. The listing would then end.

Starting price

The starting price for an auction is such a big subject that it could warrant a book on its own! There is no doubt in my mind that if the auction has a high start price, less bidders will be attracted. The possibility of a bargain will entice many to bid, hoping that they get lucky. The tricky bit is deciding at what price to start your auction.

In this section I will briefly cover some of the points to consider when setting a start price and then outline my thinking and the policy that I adopted some time ago and still use today. In the end, experience will determine the starting price policy that you use and it will be different for all eBay sellers.

Fee pricing structure

The first thing to consider when setting a start price for your items is the current eBay pricing structure that is in place. As we have discovered, the charging mechanism includes a listing fee which is applied when you submit the auction. Currently, there is a price band of £5 to £14.99 for which a fee of 35p applies. To list the item at £15 will enter the next bracket of charges and incur a fee of 75p. In this example it may be advantageous to start the auction at £14.99.

Psychology of an auction

Much has been written about the psychology involved when setting a starting price and it can be used to the seller's advantage. During your research on eBay, you may have noticed that a particular item is for sale in a conventional auction and obtained a certain price, but further down the listings you may find another auction with a fixed price for a lot less. Surely, you might think, the bidders on the first auction will stop bidding and just buy the item outright? The reality is that they probably do not know that an alternative exists. Once they have found an item that suits them, they are likely to stick with it. Of course, there are other factors involved, such as the terms and conditions of each seller, but as a general rule if you can get as many bidders as possible involved early on, your auction will do well.

Another benefit of this is that a lower price will attract more visitors. The chance of a bargain, which they might even be able to sell on, will draw them in. They will not only see the item they were originally interested in, but also any other items that you have for sale, and in particular any that you have mentioned within your description.

Natually there is the danger that the item may not attract as many bids as you expect and it could sell for a low price. This could be down to many things: a poor title, the wrong product or even just bad luck. In some cases a low start price may indicate that the item is in some way inferior – a designer handbag with a 99p start price may suggest that it is a copy, even if it is not. As a general rule I would suggest that you start your auctions at the minimum price you would be prepared to accept for the item and all you will need is just one bid. Experience will show you where it is possible to reduce the starting price in the knowledge that the item is likely to reach a much higher price.

Reserve price

The 'reserve price' option is exactly what it says and works in the same way as a reserve at a traditional auction where the minimum price you are prepared to accept is left with the auctioneer. The item will be auctioned as normal, but if the reserve price is not met the item will not be sold. eBay works on the same principles, with the exception that if there is a reserve price on an item which has not yet been reached, then 'reserve not met' will appear next to the high bid whilst the auction is in progress.

There is a fee to include a reserve price, however the advantages are that you create a safety net under your auction, just in case it proves to be unpopular. It could also demonstrate that you value the item highly and are not prepared to 'give it away'; this may also encourage bidding. The major disadvantage comes when the auction ends. If the reserve price has not been reached, the high bidder does not actually take home the prize, which is very disappointing for them.

eBay have recently introduced a lower limit for reserve prices of £50, which will have reduced the number of auctions with a reserve significantly.

Buy It Now option as well?

The next option on the auction listing is to decide if your auction will have a fixed price as well as an auction start price. This allows the bidder to buy it outright for the fixed price or to start the ball rolling by placing a bid in the traditional way. When the auction is first listed, both the option to buy outright and the option to place a bid will exist. If the visitor bids, then the 'Buy It Now' option will lapse.

There is a fee for this option, based on the value of the fixed price you use, and with some items it can work very well. Many bidders will not want to wait until the auction ends and would prefer to have the item that much quicker; this option gives them the opportunity to spend their money with you that little bit faster.

TIP Start auctions low to stimulate interest, but if there have not been any bids after a few days, revise the start price to the minimum you would be content with.

After experimenting with many different starting price options, I have settled on a standard start price policy for nearly all of the items I sell. They start at 99p with no reserve price, and the market decides the final selling price. For items that I have not tried before, or that I think will not attract many viewers, I will start the auctions at a higher price. As I have in excess of 50 auctions running at any one time, any visits I get must be good as I cross sell all of my items. The more visitors to my auctions, the better.

Sometimes an item will fall short of my expectations, but it may well have generated more sales as a 'loss-leader'. I use the 'Buy It Now' option sparingly as I am a big fan of market forces, but it can be useful when I know the figure I need to achieve or I have several items that need to be sold quickly. It can also work out a little cheaper on fees: a standard item with a 99p start price and a 'Buy It Now' option of £20 will currently cost 30p to list, whereas starting the item at £20 will cost 75p.

Applicable VAT rate included in sales price

The box for VAT rate is applicable for business sellers, it is likely that you will not need to complete this entry at the moment.

Quantity of items

As a general rule, you are likely to list only one item in an auction. If you have more than one item, you have the option to use the 'Buy it Now' fixed price format. If you have more than one item and decide not to use the fixed price, it is possible to list more than one item in a traditional auction format.

> I have not found the need to use multiple item listings as yet and have not found many in use when searching through the eBay site. If you do decide that this is the option for you, refer to the online eBay help section, which explains the process.

Multiple item listings

The rules for multiple item listings are different and take some getting used to. There is a help link next to the quantity box that will explain the process. I would suggest that unless you intend to use this method, there is not any great need to understand how it works.

Duration

The next decision to be made concerns the duration that you would like the auction to run. As the time at which the auction starts is the same time that it will end, the duration can also impact on the final price.

 TIP Telling bidders that your item does not have a reserve price may actually encourage them to bid as they will know that if they do become the highest bidder, then they will win the item.

The current options for the duration of an auction are:

- 1 day

- 3 days

- 5 days

- 7 days

- 10 days

Each option has its own advantages. A ten day auction, for example, will allow your auction to run over two weekends. If it starts on a Thursday – which is traditionally a slow day for listings – it will end ten days later on a Sunday, which is generally regarded as a good time for an auction to end. Thursdays are also the most common day for eBay to run a promotion, offering reduced fees, or even a free listing day.

Seven day auctions are the most frequently used on eBay. They are easy to track, will include one weekend and allow enough days to provide opportunity for more visits, whilst at the same time, not asking the high bidder to wait too long for their item. The three and five day auctions are also useful if you believe that most bidding occurs at the end of the auction, with maybe a little activity when the item is newly listed. This would suggest that the duration of the auction is not so important, it is the end time that really counts.

One day auctions

The one day auction is worth a little more explanation, as this can be a great duration for an auction under certain circumstances. If you have an item that has a deadline, for example theatre tickets, then the shorter auction will work. Seasonal events such as Christmas can be a very busy and profitable time for sellers; the one day format allows you to make those last few sales before the event and catch the last post before Christmas.

Perhaps the most important use of a one day auction is for those sellers who have many identical items to sell. eBay will only allow sellers to list a maximum of fifteen identical items at any one time, so if you have 100 DVDs to sell, you can only have fifteen listed each week if you choose the seven day auction. A one day auction will allow you to list 70 items in a week – just start another one when the first one ends.

Altering the duration of an auction can impact on the numbers of bids you receive. On the one hand if the item is listed for a longer period, it will gain more exposure, however a ten day auction may prove too long for some bidders to wait and they move on to an auction that ends sooner. There is no right answer. The items you sell and the experience you gain will ultimately decide which auction duration you choose.

Private buyers

As it suggests, this option gives you the option to allow your buyers to remain anonymous. As yet, I have not needed to use this facility. Although some of my auctions are a little odd, none demand anonymity.

Start time

It's standard that your auction will begin when you submit your listing and run for the duration you set. As the auction will end at the same time a few days later, the time at which you enter the auction may not be the best time for it to end. There is no perfect time for your auction to end; it will depend upon the item you sell and the market you are aiming at. However, it does seem that an end time during the evening is the most favoured. For the American market, a later finish time may prove to be better, but not in the early hours of the morning as the UK will be asleep.

NOTE

One day auctions are not currently available for 'Buy It Now' fixed price only listings.

TIP

After several years of trading, I have settled on a ten day auction format as standard. This allows me to maintain a reasonable number of active auctions without increasing my daily workload. In the run up to Christmas I will use most of the other formats to move as much stock as possible right up until the last posting date.

It is not possible to cater for the whole world, but it is possible to time your auctions so that they end when your target market is about. For example, if you are selling children's toys, then it might be a good idea to end the auction while the children are still awake, so that they can persuade their parents to make that extra bid. If it is a more adult item, maybe consumer electronics, then when the children are in bed might be the best idea so that the adults can bid without having the children around.

So, with a little thought, it is possible to list your items in a sequence so that you make the best use of the end time of your auctions. There may, however, be a problem if you are selling several items and using the traditional method to list them; there is just not enough time to complete all your listings within the optimum window of time.

To accommodate this, eBay has the option to schedule your auction start time so that it will start at a pre-determined time in the future.

Schedule start time

Using this option, you can arrange for your auction to begin anything up to three weeks in advance. Scheduled auctions start on the quarter hour, which means that you can have 13 different start times between the hours of 7pm and 10pm. The scheduling facility also allows you to check your auctions for errors before they go 'live'.

Listing whilst on holiday

The ability to schedule your listings is great if you decide to take a break, as they can start while you are away and with a little planning they can end just after you return. You can even check your email while you are away to answer questions. You may decide to stop listing before you depart in order for a sunnier climate; it would make sense to end all your auctions, leaving enough time to dispatch them before you go away.

> As the majority of items that I sell are aimed at the family market, including toys, I have found that the best time for my auctions to end is between 7pm and 10pm. I believe this is the best time for my UK customers and is just about OK for the American market as well.

Global market time zones

The scheduling facility will allow you to market to specific countries around the world, without having to actually submit auctions in the early hours of the morning. The prime time for an auction in the USA might be early evening, which could mean listing the item well into the night in the UK.

TIP If you are selling a number of items that may appeal to the same bidders, do not list them all to end at the same time, instead stagger them by 15 minutes. This will enable bidders to watch one auction end and switch to the next with enough time to spare – don't rush your bidders, let them buy at a comfortable speed.

Top tips for choosing the best start times

1. **Schedule auctions**

   Use the schedule facility when you need to: for a small fee, you will be able to list at all times of the day and even while you are on holiday.

2. **Start auctions between 7pm and 10pm**

   You can never cater for the whole world, somebody will always be asleep when your auction ends. However a finish time of between 7 and 10 in the evening should cover most of the UK markets and mid to late afternoon in the USA.

3. **End on a Sunday if possible**

   A Sunday evening should find most people at home preparing for the new week at work. Choose a time after the evening meal and then choose the actual time according to who you are targeting.

4. **Start each auction at a different time**

   Leave a reasonable amount of time between auctions to let your bidders catch their breath and return again.

5. **Avoid major events**

   Be aware of key events such as World Cup football matches or The Oscars – ending an auction in the middle of these will result in less bidding activity at the end.

 TIP When you are away on holiday or taking a break, consider a 'dummy listing' informing your regular visitors that you will be back soon, and use this to preview your next batch of auctions. This effectively will keep your shop open until you return.

Payment methods

As the title suggests, it is now time to list the payment methods you will accept. When you list a second item, these entries will be remembered by the system, so if the next item is similar, these will not need to be altered.

It is simply a case of ticking the boxes that relate to each form of payment you are prepared to accept. The current options are:

- PayPal – If you would like your payment to go into another Paypal account, just enter the email address in this box.

- Postal order/Banker's draft

- Personal cheque

- Other

- Credit cards

- Escrow

We have already looked at most of these. However 'Other' and 'Escrow' may need just a brief explanation. The option 'Other' instructs the bidder that payment options are contained within the description; you can just write your preferred payment methods and use this box to tell bidders to look in your description.

Escrow

Escrow is an eBay approved third party which will hold the payment on behalf of the buyer while they inspect the item; if they are happy then payment is released to the seller. This may be of interest for higher value items and does offer some piece of mind.

The process works as follows:

1. The buyer sends payment to the escrow company, a trusted third party.

2. The seller ships the item to the buyer.

3. The buyer inspects and approves the item.

4. Funds are paid to the seller.

As with most things, there is a charge for this service and the fee will vary according to the amount of the transaction and the method of payment.

Postage

This is the section where you will select the areas of the world that you will post to. You can select the UK only, or pick and choose regions of the world.

Domestic postage

You can either decide to offer the same postage rates to all UK buyers or not to post the item; it is difficult to bubble wrap a shed!

For those items that cannot be posted, select 'No postage: local pickup only' from the pull down menu, and then detail the arrangements either in the item description or in the 'payment instructions' box, which will be found at the end of this page. eBay will include the item location as a guide for buyers, you can alter this if required.

Services and costs

As we have already calculated the postage costs for the item, they now just need to be entered onto the system. This section is split into two main parts: the service(s) you will offer and the cost of each service. Use the pull down menu and choose up to three options, so you can quote First Class, Second Class and maybe Special Delivery.

You could if you wish offer your item with no postage costs. This might sound a little strange, but many sellers use this as part of their sales strategy and eBay have been known to offer reduced fees for items with free postage, so it may be worth considering.

International postage

This section can also have three entries, perhaps you will choose Airmail into Europe and Worldwide and a Surface mail option. These options can be changed from auction to auction and will alter according to the item you are selling. Just select your options from the menus and enter the cost for each.

There is also the option at this stage to inform your bidders about postal insurance for both domestic and international services; you may insist on this for certain items or leave it as optional. A big improvement on the original selling form is the option to offer a different insurance fee to international buyers.

Item location

The item location will be very important for items that need to be collected. Give your buyers as much information as possible before they make the buying decision.

Buyer requirements

You have the option to impose restrictions on the type of bidders you will accept. If you want to apply any, click the link and a menu of options will appear. I currently opt to block buyers who are registered in countries to which I don't post and who have 2 'Unpaid Item' strikes in the last 30 days. This is an attempt to cut down on the number of non-payers I receive.

Keep the list of buyer requirements as low as you can as too many will restrict your potential customer base.

Return policy

In this space you can provide details of your returns policy – you may already have given this some thought in an earlier chapter. Business sellers may well have additional legal obligations as we have already discussed.

An example of a standard return policy might read: "We aim to provide the highest levels of quality and service. If we do make a mistake, please let us know and we will do all we can to put things right. If your purchase is not as you had expected, just return it in it's original condition and packaging within 14 days and we will be happy to provide a full refund, including the original postage costs."

Additional checkout instructions

These instructions will appear in your final listing as 'Seller's Payment Instructions'. This is a great place to mention anything that you think may benefit a potential bidder. You could specify your local pick-up details, provide details of how often you post items, or anything else you can think of.

 TIP As mentioned before, enter as much postal information at this stage as possible – it will cut down on the number of emails you receive.

My Payment Instructions currently read:

"INTERNATIONAL AIRMAIL SHIPPING RATES ARE SHOWN ABOVE.

Shipping costs include all stamps, packing materials, boxes, bubble bags, wrapping and so on. We promise:- Fast Shipping, - Top class Packaging, - Great communications."

These are not necessarily what you would expect to find. I am using the space to aid my sales by offering a 'customer promise'.

Stage 3: Promote and review your listing

This is the final stage in the listing process. It allows you to review your listing and make any changes that might be required. eBay take the opportunity to offer additional services (for a fee) which will enhance the look and visibility of your item.

Make your listing stand out

You may well have already selected the gallery option and may even have opted for a subtitle; you now have the option to spend even more money.

Gallery Plus

This option will show your gallery picture in a larger size if a viewer hovers over it with their mouse.

Bold

The 'Bold' option adds emphasis to your listings with a darker title, as shown below.

Fig 12. Bold listing

Highlight

The 'Highlight' option emphasises your listing with a coloured band.

Fig 13. Highlighted listing

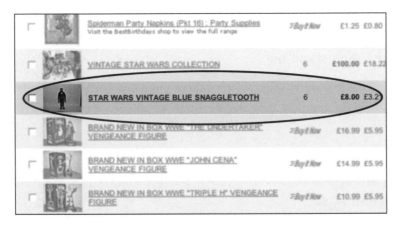

Featured Plus

This option gives your listing prominent placement in the category list and search results. Your item will be shown in the Featured Items section of the category list that you select for your item.

Fig 14. Featured category listing

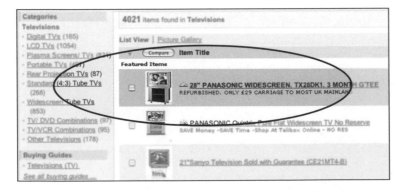

Gallery Featured

Using 'Gallery Featured' ensures your item will periodically appear in the special Featured section above the general Gallery. Your picture will be almost double the size of non-featured Gallery pictures, and will also appear in the general Gallery.

Home Page Featured

With 'Home Page Featured', your listing has a chance to rotate in a special display on eBay's home page. There are additional charges for each of these options, so you will have to decide if your item is worth the extra investment.

Your item will also stand out in the search result list. Each search results page has a Featured Items section at the top of the page – your item will be featured in this list.

Fig 15. Featured in search result lists

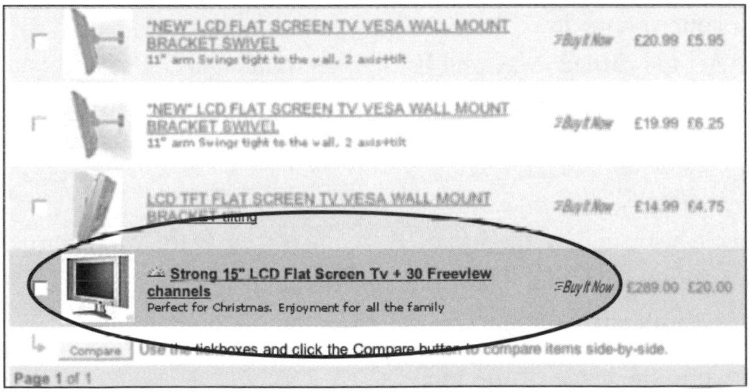

Stage 4: Review your listing

The final section in the listing process will allow you to check your whole auction section by section to make sure that the information is correct. If any aspects do require amending, use the 'edit' links to the right hand side and make your changes.

The description will now be shown as your bidders will see it. If you wrote the page in HTML, this may be the first time you see it in its full glory.

Finally, when you have checked all the details, click the 'submit' button. As soon as you submit your auction, eBay will raise charges for the listing of the item.

Although you have now listed, or scheduled, your first auction, you can still amend and add to it while it is live on the system. The next section will demonstrate some of things you can still do.

Recommendations for the first few auctions

1. **Keep your volume low**
   Don't get too carried away and list dozens of auctions all at once; there will be issues around packing and you may copy mistakes from one auction to another. Start slow and learn as you go.

2. **Keep it simple**
   To begin with, follow the basic eBay process for listing, use the standard template and learn the processes before getting too involved with advanced auction design.

3. **Relative to the value of the item**
   Don't spend loads of time designing a description and layout for a low value item. While it is important to create the right atmosphere, you must consider the amount of time it will take and balance this against your return.

4. **Take time to review each auction**
   Use the final stage to double check that your postage rates are correct, you have selected the best category and so on.

Summary

You should now know:

- how to best select **categories** for your items;
- how to best describe your items in the **title and description** fields;
- what **starting price** to set;
- how the **reserve price** works;
- how to select the **duration** of your auction;
- what **start time** to choose;
- what **picture** options you have;
- how to improve the **visibility** of your item on eBay listings;
- how to set the **payment and postage** options; and finally
- how important it is to carefully **review** your listing before going live.

Congratulations, your first auction should now be live!

But you're not finished yet. You can make changes to your auctions while they are live – which is the subject of the next chapter.

5

During the auction

Overview

There are several things that may happen whilst your auction is in progress, this section outlines some of them. You may receive emails from bidders asking questions about your item, or where you live, how much the postage is and so on, but you may also wish to make some changes to your auction.

The number of amendments you can make will reduce if the item has received a bid, so you may not always be able to alter what was placed in the original auction. However, the seller does retain control during the period that the auction is live. The options below are the most common and are the ones you are likely to need to manage your auctions.

Revise your item

Once an item has been listed, it can still be revised; perhaps you need to correct errors, or add further information. The process is different if a bid has already been placed.

Before a bid

To revise your item before any bids have been placed, the best place to start is 'my eBay':

1. Click 'selling'.

2. Select the item you wish to revise.

3. In the top section, click 'revise your item'.

4. Click 'continue'.

5. Click on the 'edit link' of the section you wish to alter.

6. Make amendments as required.

7. Click 'save changes'.

8. Review the listing and submit revisions.

After a bid

When your item has received a bid, you can no longer edit all of the details. You will not be able to edit the title or existing description and the postage rates are now fixed. You can, however, still make some additions, and it can prove very useful, the process is very similar to the 'before a bid' process:

1. From 'my eBay' click selling.

2. Select the item you wish to revise.

3. In the top section, click 'revise your item'.

4. Click 'continue'.

5. Click on the section you wish to add information in.

6. Make amendments as required.

7. Click 'save changes'.

8. Review the listing and submit revisions.

Cancelling a bid

You may be asked to cancel a bid that has been placed in error. The bidder can retract the bid themselves, but often through inexperience they cannot do so and within the last few hours they cannot retract anyway. If a bid has been placed in error and the bidder has no intention of completing the trade, it is in your interest to remove it as soon as possible so that the price falls back to where it was before they placed their bid. This new low price may encourage renewed interest.

You may of course decide to remove a bid because you are not happy with the bidder. Perhaps their feedback is not good enough or you have stipulated a minimum feedback score as a bidding criteria, which they do not meet. If you wish to cancel a bid, as with all things on eBay, there is a process to be followed:

1. View the item in question.

2. Select the bid history.

3. Note the ID of the bidder.

4. Copy the item number.

5. Click 'services' from the top menu.

6. Click 'cancel bids'.

7. Enter your password.

8. Enter item number and User ID.

9. Choose reason for cancelling the bids.

10. Click cancel bid – note that all bids by this user will be removed, not just the highest bid.

11. Email bidder to confirm the removal.

> The strangest bid I have had on one of my auctions occurred during the auction of my car when I had a bid placed from a user registered in India. I had to cancel their bid. Although I was prepared to deliver the car a reasonable distance, there are limits!

End a listing early

There may be some occasions where you will want to end your listing early. Perhaps the item is no longer for sale, it may have become damaged or the listing was incorrect and can no longer be revised due to bids being placed.

Ending auctions early will upset bidders and if is it done on a regular basis, they may not return to your site. Auctions should not be ended early just because the price is not high enough; it may well rise at the end anyway. The process to end an auction is as follows:

1. View the auction you want to cancel.

2. Copy the item number.

3. Click 'services' from the top menu.

4. Click 'End your listing early'.

5. Enter your password.

6. Enter the auction number.

7. Click continue.

8. Choose reason for cancelling.

9. Click 'end your listing'.

Selling directly

You could of course receive an offer for your item and decide to remove it from eBay and make the sale directly to the buyer. Unsurprisingly, eBay, do not approve of this as they will not be able to charge any final value fees for the item. On the face of it, this is a good idea from the seller's perspective as they will save some money by avoiding the 'end of auction' fees. However, in the longer term, maintaining a good relationship with eBay is worth much more.

Trading outside of the eBay system is not necessarily a good idea as it leads to a loss of protection for both the buyer and seller, and the normal feedback rules do not apply. If you do decide to accept a fixed price from a bidder whilst the auction is underway, there are two ways to achieve this and stay within the rules.

1. If the item has not yet had a bid, place a 'Buy It Now' (BIN) option on the listing by using the 'Revise Your Item' process and inform the bidder that you have done so. They can then visit the auction and purchase immediately.

2. If the item has received a bid, the option to add a 'BIN' price will lapse. If this is the case, cancel your listing, then re-list it with the same start price (this should result in a credit for the original listing fee). Include a BIN price as agreed with your preferred bidder. To deter others from bidding, title the auction badly and they will not find it. Finally let your bidder know the new item number and they should be able to buy the item as normal.

Reply to email

During the auction, you are likely to receive emails from interested eBay members who may ask any number of questions. The email from the eBay member will be sent on a form which will give you the option to 'respond' as opposed to just replying as you would normally. If you do respond, both the question and your answer will appear at the bottom of your auction, just be careful of how you word your response.

TIP If you do receive a question from an overseas eBay member, consider replying in their own language. I have found that this is very well received and might just encourage them to bid for my item. There are several language translators on the internet – you may already have included a link to one from your listing pages as we discussed earlier

Sample reply template

Construct a signature within your email program that resembles an answer to a typical question about postage costs. This can then be amended quickly and save a considerable amount of time. If you use Outlook Express, for example, your signature could look something like this:

Hi

Thanks for your note and interest in the _____ .

The airmail shipping would be £_____ . Surface mail would be about half this amount.

Hope this helps

Best wishes

_____

Each time you reply to a question, this signature will appear – just type the item into the first space and the cost into the second space and hit the send button. This will save loads of time compiling emails. This email template can also be used to promote your sales activities by incorporating live links, which I will cover in a later section.

> I once received an email from a new eBayer member which included a screen print of his bid confirmation page, which they believed I would need as proof of their bid. This page showed the maximum amount of their bid, which was higher than the current auction value. I replied, suggesting that they should not send this kind of information as it would be quite possible (although not allowed), to bump up the price to their maximum bid. No reply back from the bidder, and in time they were out bid anyway.

First auction completed

That is your first auction completed. Now just sit back and wait for the bidders to visit the auction and if it is the right item at the right time, and you have entered the correct details, it should sell and mark the beginning of your online business.

If the process in this last chapter has worked for you, stick with it. There is no need to make things more complicated or involved if you are happy with the result. If, after a few more auctions, you feel that you could make some changes to the auction, maybe add more pictures or use a different design, then the next few chapters will show you some of the ways that these changes can be made and what kind of results you can expect to achieve.

I'll end this chapter with five tips for creating successful auctions.

The top five tips for successful auctions

1. **Create a friendly sales environment**
   People buy from people (I might have mentioned this before – but it bears repeating!) Create an auction where bidders will feel happy to do business; if it is hostile and threatening, many will move on.

2. **Welcome new users**
   New eBay members are great, they can become very excited and will bid far more than they intended. Welcome them to your auctions.

3. **Be aware of page load times**
   If your auction takes too long to load, bidders will move on. Appeal to as many potential customers as possible, don't force them away before they have even seen your item.

4. **Keep the content to a reasonable amount**
   Long pages full of tedious detail will put bidders off, they just will not read it. Bidders will see many auctions, and you need to tell them in the first few words and with your picture, why they should bid on your item. Do not bore the customer.

5. **Adopt a consistent design format**
   A consistent site design from the beginning will make your workload much easier and any repeat visitors will know what to expect. Plan it well and stick to it.

Summary

You should now:

- know how to **revise elements** of your item during an auction;

- understand what can, and cannot be done, before and after the **first bid**;

- know how to **cancel** a bid;

- know how to **end a listing early**;

- understand why it is not a good idea to **sell direct** to a bidder outside of eBay; and

- know how to reply efficiently to **email questions**.

Even though I've now sold over 6,000 items on eBay, I still find the closing stages of auctions exciting! Will the price surge in the closing seconds...? However, after the auction has ended, there is work to do – which is what we look at in the next chapter.

After the auction

Overview

When the auction ends, several things will happen almost at once. First, you will receive an email notifying you that the auction has ended and whether the item sold. The buyer will receive an invoice informing them that they were the highest bidder. Several aspects of the auction listing will also change and you will be able to view the particulars of the trade and now see the buyers email address and they can see yours. The email that the seller receives will have the option to send information to the buyer. It will also have links to the item and a summary of the final details including the postage costs.

The buyer will receive an email that also includes a summary of the trade. It may also contain a link to pay immediately or to request information from the seller.

The information about the sale can be sent in several ways and you must anticipate that the buyer may contact you through a variety of means. You may also decide to send an invoice to the buyer, which they will receive in addition to the automatic invoice email generated by eBay.

How things progress from this point will depend upon how the buyer intends to pay and how quickly they respond; they may of course be interested in more of your auctions

The main point is that a contract has been agreed between the buyer and seller and as long as the buyer has all the necessary information, payment should be the next stage.

Second chance offer

The 'second chance offer' facility allows the seller to make a direct offer to any under-bidders of a completed auction. The seller can make an offer to the third or fourth placed bidder if the bid price was high enough and, of course, they have the stock.

How it works

The second chance offer allows the seller to make an offer to any under-bidders at their highest bid price. This offer does not incur any listing fees, but the final value fee will still apply if the under-bidder accepts the offer. All the details of the original auction still apply, so this option only works if you have more than one identical item. The under-bidder will receive an email containing the offer, which includes instructions on how to accept it.

The offer can remain active for a number of days, which you can decide. If you want to re-list the item soon, only make the offer for one day; if you are not in a hurry to re-list, extend the offer for more days.

When to use it

If any of the under-bids are at or above your expected price for the item, then the second chance option is a great way to increase your turnover. It will also remove the need to place a separate listing for the extra items, which means that you can list something else instead.

When sending a second chance offer, remember that the bidder may not have access to their email all of the time. They may bid from work on a Friday and not pick up the email until the Monday morning, by which time it may be too late to accept it.

> I have found that second chance offers that are made immediately after the auction ends are more likely to be taken by the bidder. The second and third placed bidders may only just have been out bid and given the chance to buy another, they may well accept. Whereas, over time the interest in the item will fade.

Receiving payment

This is the best part of having your own eBay business – watching the money roll in!

Payments will arrive in the manner that you stipulated in your payment options section. Well, they should! You will, however, find that you receive payments in a variety of methods you did not expect, and these may even be in different currencies.

The more payment options you offer to your bidders, the more processes you must have in place to cater for them. If you accept personal cheques, it is worth contacting your bank and agreeing a limit as to how many you can clear through a personal cheque account. Business accounts may incur a fee for clearing cheques.

It is prudent to allow any form of payment to clear before sending the item. Cheques and electronic cheques do take several days to clear and there is a chance that some payments will be recovered from your PayPal account.

> Over the past two years I have sent all items on receipt of payment, I do not wait for clearance. I am not suggesting that this is the best way to run a business; my average sale price is just £10, and I may clear a larger payment. In all this time I have only had two cheques bounce, but there have been loads with the wrong date, unsigned, or made out to my eBay ID which did confuse my bank just a little.

Late payment excuses

Not surprisingly, payment doesn't always come in quickly and smoothly. You have to be flexible. Some of the excuses I've received are:

"I am sorry, I didn't realise that I had won the auction."

"An in-law placed the bid and has now died."

"Sorry, I didn't realise you are in the UK."

"Sorry for the late payment, there was a power cut and I couldn't check my e-mail."

But my favourite excuse is:

"Sorry for the late payment, I was stung by a wasp."

Packaging

Packing up your items can be a tedious job, and as your turnover increases, it will become worse. If you gave some thought to the packing before you listed the auction, you will already know how it will be packaged and should have the materials to hand.

If you sell the same type of item all of the time, then the packing will not require much thought. For example, if you sell lots of DVDs, you may find that a standard bubble bag will cater for up to three discs and one parcel is much like the next. If you sell a range of items of differing size, you may even end up making the boxes.

TIP Only pack up the item after the auction ends, as buyers quite often purchase more than one item over a period of days. You do not want to unpack it in order to send with something else.

Overseas parcels

Sending parcels overseas is much the same as sending them in the UK. The actual packaging should be the same, although it might be an idea to use better adhesive tape if sending by surface mail as the package needs to stay in one piece for longer.

The main differences are in the information required on the parcel. If you are using an international carrier for large parcels, they will have the necessary documentation; if using the standard Royal Mail services, a few simple additions to the package will be sufficient.

Generally, the item will be either a 'small packet' or 'printed papers'. Just write the appropriate entry in the top left corner and, if sending by airmail, use a blue sticker which are available from the Post Office.

For parcels being sent outside of the EU, a customs declaration is also required. These are now white stickers. The information on this sticker includes the weight, value and a description of the contents. You will also need to sign and date the declaration.

Multiple purchases

If your buyer purchases more than one item, it would make sense to send them in one parcel; it saves you time and should save the buyer a little on postage. Check with the buyer that is what they would like to do as the delivery time may increase if the larger package is to be sent by parcel post.

 TIP When refunding excess postage charges, wherever possible use the refund process within PayPal as you will also recover some of the original fees on the payment.

Five things to avoid when packing

1. **Don't allow fragile items to touch other contents**
   It sounds like common sense, and it is. The hassle that broken items can cause is amazing, particularly if they are expensive. Use extra bubble wrap to make sure they travel well.

2. **Don't send items without the full address including post or zip code**
   If a parcel can get lost, it will, and it always seems to be overseas. Some international addresses are quite complex and we are not used to the format; get as much information about the address as possible.

3. **Don't use cheap adhesive tape**
   Some parcels may be in the system for some weeks, and it has been known for them to start to come apart. Now I use better tape for certain destinations!

4. **Don't allow items to move within the packaging**
   Use the correct packaging for the item and make sure it is secure.

5. **Don't use inferior or damaged packaging**
   Avoid cutting corners with your packaging materials. Lightweight boxes and inadequate quality packing could cost you money and the goodwill of your buyer.

Dispatch

Sending your parcels can also be a time consuming process. Queuing in the Post Office is not a good use of your time. Instead, see if your local postal depot will accept parcels, or if you have sufficient quantity, it may be worth arranging for them to be collected. Parcels

> To save time when sending parcels, I purchase postage stamps directly from Royal Mail and weigh and stamp my own parcels. I also fill in my proof of postage certificate before I send my parcels.

sent by most couriers are usually collected, which will save a journey.

Proof of posting

When using the standard Royal Mail service, you can obtain a 'proof of postage', which confirms that the item has been sent to the correct address. It is also date stamped by the issuer. This certificate is free and if the parcel is lost or damaged, it will help any claim for compensation and also proves that the item was posted.

Notify buyer

When the item has been sent, send the buyer an email informing them that it is in the post and give an idea of how long it should take to arrive. Use this note to thank them for their custom and invite them back to your site.

TIP To cut down on time when sending these emails, write one note, copy the text and for the next item use the same format, just change the item name.

Re-list your unsold item

Some of your items may not sell; maybe the item had a high start price or was not listed correctly, or for one of many other reasons. eBay would obviously like you to sell the item so that they can recover the final value fee, so they will allow you to re-list the item for sale and will not charge the normal listing fee. You can re-list an unsold item only once for free; if it doesn't sell the second time round, you will have to pay the standard listing fee.

To re-list the same item again for the same price and with the same description, simply go to your 'my eBay' page, and click on the 'Unsold' link. There will be a re-list option to the right side of the page, click this, scroll down the page and click 'submit listing'.

You can, however, change almost every aspect of your auction, by using the 'edit' links before you submit. As it did not sell the first time, it would probably be worth changing something: maybe the title, starting price or even the day that the auction will finish. In order to qualify for the free listing entry, the start price must be equal to or less than the price it was the first time; this is the actual price you used, not the price band that it fell into.

If you decide not to re-list the actual item that didn't sell, you can still qualify for a free re-list and sell a completely different item. Just change all the details of the auction, ensuring that the start price is the same, or lower, than the original item.

> When I agree to a direct sale with a buyer, I will use an unsold item, re-list it as above with the details of the new trade and inform them of the new item number. I will incur the final value fees as usual, but will receive a credit for the actual listing fee. It all helps.

Claiming back fees

Sometimes your high bidder will, for whatever reason, not complete the sale and not pay for the item. These are known as 'Non-Paying Bidders' or 'Non-Paying Buyers'. As the trade did not complete, it is not right that the seller should still pay the final value fee. eBay have a process which will allow the seller to reclaim these fees and at the same time issue a warning to the bidder who didn't pay.

The reasons for non-payment vary and the eBay process will allow you to select the reason why the trade did not end with a satisfactory conclusion.

> Over a two year period I have had about 1% of my bidders not pay. In each case I have reclaimed my eBay fees, even if it was just a few pence.

Non-paying buyer

How long you decide to wait for payment may depend upon the type of auction, where the buyer is in the world, how much feedback they have, or you may have settled on a policy which sets out your payment timescales.

The non-paying buyer (NPB) process has one main objective, which is to claim back your end of auction fees from eBay. During the process, the high bidder will be sent an email reminding them to pay and telling them of the consequences. Often this note from eBay will prompt them into paying, so it is definitely worth completing.

If your high bidder still does not complete the trade, they will be given a warning from eBay. With three of these warnings, their account will be suspended and they will become 'NARU' (not a registered user). If their feedback score was high, this is usually a good deterrent as they will have to start again with zero feedback. If your high bidder has become NARU since your auction ended, you should be able to reclaim your fees straightaway.

> I usually wait until one week after the auction ends and if I have not heard from the high bidder, I will send a polite email asking if all is OK and offering assistance. The high bidder may have forgotten about the item, or be on holiday, so I give them a gentle reminder. If another week passes with no contact, I will begin the 'Non-Paying Buyer' process (NPB).

The process to complete the NPB process is as follows:

1. Start at 'my eBay'.

2. Click 'sold items' and open the item.

3. Copy the item number.

4. Select 'services' from the top menu.

5. Click 'Report an unpaid item'.

6. Paste the item number into the box.

7. Click 'continue'.

8. Choose a reason from the list.

9. Select a statement that best describes what has happened so far in the dispute.

10. Click 'continue'.

11. Click 'send an unpaid item reminder'.

When you have sent your reminder, the high bidder will be sent an email. They can then respond to the reminder, or pay, or do nothing. You can, at any time, view your disputes and you will be prompted by eBay if your action is required. There are three outcomes to a disputed auction:

1. The bidder pays for the item. Both parties are satisfied and the dispute is closed by you the seller. You will not receive a fee refund and the bidder will not get a non-payer strike.

2. The bidder does not respond and after a period of time you decide not to wait any longer. You will receive a refund and the bidder will receive one non-payer strike.

3. Both parties have decided not to complete the transaction for whatever reason. When the bidder confirms this to eBay, you will receive a refund and they will not incur a non-payer item strike.

Unless your non-payer item strike is the third for your bidder and they are suspended, they will still be able to leave you feedback on the transaction, which is something to be aware of when you leave comments about them in the dispute forum.

Summary

You should now know:

- when to make a **second chance** offer;

- that in general, it's better to wait for **payments to clear** before dispatching items;

- how best to **package** your items;

- how to send packages **overseas**;

- how to re-list **unsold items**;

- how to **claim back fees** from eBay; and

- how to deal with a **non-paying buyer**.

Hopefully, you've now sold your first item. In the next chapter we will look at ways to improve the format of your auctions to make them more attractive to buyers.

Refining your auction format

Overview

The basic auction format that we have discussed has introduced you to the mechanics of eBay and demonstrated how an auction is placed and also how almost anything can sell on eBay.

You may now have some ideas of how you would like to improve things. Perhaps you have seen other auctions with more pictures, or links to other pages.

The extent of any changes that you choose to make is down to personal choice. These changes can be made using HTML, or by using the standard method of listing your auction.

This chapter builds on the basic entry of an auction and shows some of the ways that you can make changes. Experiment with some of them; if they work for you, then great, if they are not what you had in mind, then just revert back to the standard method.

Over time, my auction site design has changed many times and will certainly do so again in the future. For now, I have settled on a standard format which consists of:

- A border around the description.

- A plain single coloured background.

- One large picture within the description which is 640 by 480 pixels.

- Two cross-sell links with small pictures to my other auctions.

- Links to an extra web page where I show additional pictures.

- A link to additional web pages which contain my details and trading terms.

I feel that using links for additional information leaves the auction uncluttered and will allow it to load quicker. The border around the listing saves me money on the eBay listing designers and the large pictures save me buying super-size pictures from eBay. As the seasons change, so I will alter the look of the site, with a Christmas or Easter theme, or maybe just when I feel like a change.

Standard method

Improving the look of your auctions does not necessarily involve complicated technical knowledge of computers and HTML code. There are several things that can be done just using the 'copy' and 'paste' functions, and a few simple codes which are shown below. It must be stressed, that if you are happy with the way your auctions look, stick with it; only refine them when you want to achieve something a bit different.

First, we will look at two computer techniques that can make your life a lot easier.

Two tips

1. Copy and paste

To effect these changes to your auction format, you will need to master the copy and paste functions on your computer. If this is new to you, these few lines should help (note: this applies to Windows, but a similar technique also applies for Macs and other systems).

The basic operation of copy and paste involves three stages:

1. **Highlight text**
   Identify the text that you would like to copy. Highlight it by placing your mouse at the beginning of the text, then hold down your left mouse button and drag your mouse to the end of the text, and then release the left mouse button. The text should now be highlighted.

2. **Copy the text onto the clipboard**
   Hover your mouse over the text and click your right mouse button. A pop-up menu will appear, from which you select 'copy'.

3. **Paste the text where you want it**
   Select the new location where you would like the text to appear, click the right button again and click 'paste'.

Practice with this until it becomes easy and you will then be ready to make some design changes to your auctions.

References

www.webmasternow.com/copyandpaste.html
www.worldstart.com/tips/shared/copypaste.htm

2. Opening a second browser window

There are many situations where it is useful to open more than one browser window. For example, you might be reading a long article on Polish needlework, when you want to quickly check the latest test score. You want to look at the BBC website to find out the score, but you don't want to lose the fascinating stitching article. This is where opening two browser windows can be helpful.

There are two simple ways to open two (or indeed multiple) windows:

1. If you are reading a web page and you want to click on a link, but you do not want to lose the current web page, hold the 'Shift' key down while clicking on the link. Hey presto, a new browser window will open, with the linked to page loaded in it.

2. If you want a new blank browser window, from the top menu bar select File > New > Window. A new window will open and you can input any URL you want.

Having opened two or more browser windows, you can switch between them either by clicking the tabs in the task bar at the bottom of the screen, or pressing the keys Alt and Tab.

NOTE The above refers to Internet Explorer on MS Windows, but the technique works similarly with other browsers and operating systems.

Inserts

We discussed the use of *inserts* in an earlier chapter and used them to add the standard eBay inserts of 'sellers other items' and 'add to favourites list'. It is possible to create your own inserts; eBay allow up to five personal inserts to be created.

These extra inserts can be used for:

1. Terms and conditions for multiple products.

2. Standard signature.

3. Links to other eBay pages.

4. Links to external web pages.

5. Links to externally hosted pictures.

These are explained in more detail below.

The list of insert types is very long, but we will only concentrate on these five as they are the ones I feel have the most benefit for this book and will give a good indication of how this facility can be used. The process is very similar to the one we have already used: just click on 'inserts', then 'create an insert', which will open in a new window.

Name your insert and then write the HTML code or text that you wish to include. You have a maximum space of 1,000 characters. Then just click 'save' and you will be able to enter your insert into the description wherever you wish.

To start with, just test the process and see how it could work for you.

1. Terms and conditions for multiple products

Perhaps you sell three different types of item, with each one needing a separate summary of trading terms, delivery times, packing details and so on. Just create three inserts and call them product A, product B, and product C, enter the specific details for each and just select the insert you need for the auction you are running.

2. Standard signature

In much the same way as the above, you could use an insert to create a signature that could be inserted anywhere within the description.

3. Links to other eBay pages

Links to other eBay pages can be included using the inserts facility. It involves a very basic use of HTML code, although you do not need to understand how it works – just copy this code into the insert box and name it 'eBay home page':

```
<a href="http://www.ebay.co.uk/">eBay home page</a>
```

This simple code will place a link in your auction which will read 'eBay home page'; it can be clicked by the bidder and will take them to the eBay home page. I should not think that many bidders would find this a tempting link and it will not really improve your sales; however, if the insert directed them to your About Me page, or your eBay shop, or another of your auctions, or maybe to the eBay registration page which might encourage 'newbies' to register and bid, then maybe it would be worth trying.

All that has to be done is to amend the HTML code shown above. It has two sections:

1. The text you would like to show in your description that they can click on (e.g. 'eBay home page').

2. The **address** of the page you wish to send the bidders to (e.g. 'http://www.ebay.co.uk/').

In the example above, 'eBay home page' is the link text that would appear on the web page, but just replace this text with 'My great DVD auction' or whatever you are selling at the time. The address would then need changing (in the example it is 'http://www.ebay.co.uk/').

A simple way to replace the address is:

1. Open a second browser window.

2. Load the target page you want (e.g. your DVD auction).

3. Highlight the address of the page (that appears in the location bar at the top of the browser window) and copy this into the clipboard.

4. Switch back to your original browser window, and paste the address in place of http://www.ebay.co.uk/ in the code.

5. Give it a new name (e.g. 'DVD auction') and it is ready for use.

The first time you do this, it will take a while, but if you have many items that you wish to promote, this is the way to do it. Experiment and see if it works for you.

4. Links to external web pages

In much the same way as above, it is possible to create links to external web pages. eBay have rules that govern the use of links from your listings. For the full list of rules, visit eBay: click on 'Help' in the top menu, then click the 'A-Z Index', click on 'L', then 'Links (Policy).'

The main use for this external linking is to an extra page that contains further details of the item for sale. If, for example, you are selling a car, the detailed description could be quite long, especially if you want to include a number of extra pictures. The load time of the item page may put off some bidders who will move on before it is fully loaded. Instead, consider a standard description, with maybe a couple of pictures, and then a link to an extra web page containing your detailed comments. This would allow the page to load quicker for all bidders and those who really want to know more can follow the link and will be prepared for the page to load.

This technique does require additional web space, which you may have from your ISP, or you may subscribe to a hosting company.

The method is the same as for 'links to other eBay pages', just include the address of your extra page between the two sets of quotes. For example:

```
<a href="http://www.yourname.f2s.com/ebay/car.htm">More
details</a>
```

You can create links to currency converters, language translators and even the parcel carrier sites by following this method. For example:

```
<a href="http://finance.yahoo.com/currency">Yahoo currency
converter</a>
```

```
<a href="http://babelfish.altavista.com/babelfish/tr">Babelfish
language translator</a>
```

5. Links to externally hosted pictures

This facility is one of the most interesting enhancements that can be made to your auction listing. Instead of just the one standard size picture hosted by eBay, or additional pictures hosted by eBay at a cost, how about having as many extra pictures as you want – which can be as large as you like – with no extra charges?

Traditionally, this has only been possible with an understanding of HTML codes. However, it can be achieved by using the copy and paste functions and the inserts facility, which we have already discussed.

There are several hosting companies on the internet which will allow you to upload your pictures for free. For example,

www.photobucket.com

www.tinypic.com

are easy to use and very popular within the eBay community. To find out what other services are currently available, just ask the question on the community discussion boards: 'How do I find a free picture hosting company?'

These companies will allocate you an amount of web space for storing pictures. They do not charge for this service, and once loaded onto the site, pictures can be placed inside your eBay listings. There is likely to be a restriction on the amount of bandwidth that can be used to view your pictures. When you create a shortcut to a picture within your listing, each time the page is viewed, the internet browser will contact the host server and display the picture. This process uses up bandwidth at the server end (which they have to pay for). The more people that look at your auctions, the more bandwidth is used. Photobucket.com will allow 1.5GB of bandwidth in any one month. If exceeded, they will disable the linking facility, something that I discovered to my detriment once.

I cannot go into great detail about the process of opening an account with every free picture hosting company as there may be dozens that I do not even know about, and each may have a slightly different way of operating. However,

> Although I use a different web hosting company for my pictures, I also use Photobucket.com from time to time.

once created, the process of loading a picture to their site is exactly the same as that used for the eBay pictures; you just browse your computer for the picture and then upload it.

The process to open an account with Photobucket.com, and to use it to host your images, couldn't be easier. Just put the kettle on and follow the steps below.

Visit www.photobucket.com and click on the 'Join Now' link. You will need to create a user name (most people just use their eBay ID), and enter the usual personal details. A confirmation email will be sent, follow the instructions and your account will be active.

When you log in to your account you will see quite a few advertisements (which is how Photobucket.com is funded) and a picture upload section that resembles the one used on eBay. The first thing to do is to load a picture from your computer. As with eBay pictures, just click Browse, locate the picture on your computer and click Submit. Photobucket.com will now copy the picture into your account.

 TIP If you are going to use lots of pictures, create a number of sub-folders to make finding them on Photobucket.com that much easier. I file my pictures with sub-folders for the month and then the day within the month.

Once you have loaded a picture into Photobucket.com, it is ready to be used in your eBay listing – just one small line of HTML code to copy and paste. Under each picture are three boxes with codes in them. They will look like a foreign language if you have not seen HTML before, but it is not important that you know what they mean at this stage. The middle box is called *Tag* and it is the contents of this box that need to be copied. It will look something like this:

```
<img src="http://img.photobucket.com/albums/v260/
youruserid/yourpicture.jpg" alt="Image hosted by
Photobucket.com">
```

Once you have copied the codes, they can be pasted directly into an eBay listing. This is done at the 'Titles & Description' stage. This section of the eBay listing is where you will describe your item. As we have seen, this can be done via a standard method using the inserts function or you can 'enter your own HTML'. If you select the HTML option, you will see your listing in HTML format, which can look very daunting. Trial and error will determine the best place to insert the codes and load in your picture. There is a whole chapter on HTML following, so don't worry too much about it now.

Pictures

How big should my pictures be?

When using the eBay picture service, pictures are edited into the available space on the system. If you choose to load your own pictures into your auctions, you can decide how big they will be.

> I have found that a picture size of 640 pixels by 480 pixels fits into a standard computer monitor screen. Anything bigger would require a horizontal scroll bar to see the whole picture and the secret is to get the visitor to do as little as possible to see your auction.

Remember: large pictures may mean that some bidders will move on to another page before the pictures are fully loaded, or the bidder may not be able to see the whole picture if their computer monitor is old or small.

Resolution refers to the number of pixels, measured horizontally and vertically, that a computer monitor uses to display text and graphics on the screen. The most common screen resolutions used on computers are:

- 640 by 480 pixels (only used by very old or small computers)

- 800 by 600 pixels

- 1024 by 768 pixels

A 640 by 480 picture would completely fill a screen of the same size, but appear smaller within a larger screen.

If you load your pictures into your description at a size of 1024 x 768 pixels, and the viewer has a screen size of 800 x 600 pixels, they will not be able to see the whole picture on their screen.

TIP If you are loading images to your own web space, edit the size of them before uploading. This will save on web hosting charges as you will be able to store more pictures.

Picture location

Each picture you store on the internet will have a unique address, which pinpoints exactly where it is. Using this address (or 'URL') we can include it on our item page by using a small piece of HTML code:

```
<img src="the address of your picture is in here">
```

For example:

```
<img src="http://www.yourname.f2s.com/ebay/photos/car.jpg">
```

As before, you do not need to know how the code works; it might take a little practice but once mastered the same process is used over and over again.

Loading your extra pictures into the listing

Before we can load the extra pictures into the listing, it helps to have two browsers open: one showing the item description that you are working on and the second with the free picture hosting site, so that you can see the picture you need.

To load your extra pictures into the listing, you will again use the inserts facility and, as before, you will create an insert and name it 'picture' and copy this code into the text space:

```
<img src=" ">
```

You now need to place the URL of your picture between the quotes. This begins 'http' and ends with '.jpg'. Just copy this from the hosting site and paste it into the code. Now click 'save'.

On the item description page, decide where you would like to add your picture, click inserts and then 'picture' and it will appear. Your new picture may appear to be huge, as there is no restriction on size; it may be too big, and need editing before it is loaded to the hosting site.

 TIP Remember to still load the first free picture into the eBay system as normal. It is this picture that will be used should you choose to use the gallery feature.

To load a second picture, open the insert called 'picture' again and replace the address with that of the new picture, then save. Now when you add the insert to your description, the second picture will appear.

If you have saved your pictures with the naming convention we discussed earlier in this book, you will only need to change the last part of the file name. For example:

- Picture 1: brownshoes-left.jpg

- Picture 2: brownshoes-right.jpg

- Picture 3: brownshoes-sole.jpg

Your own HTML

 Writing your own HTML code is not difficult, but it may look a little scary when coming across it for the first time. Take it at your own pace, it will build in a logical way.

The previous section showed how it is possible to load links and pictures into your auction without using much HTML code. This is very useful, but the method is quite limited. Entering your own HTML directly into the auction can produce some great designs.

HTML codes

This book cannot cover all of the elements of HTML code, the subject is huge, it will instead provide a few simple codes that can be used in auctions now. Hopefully, these ideas will encourage you to learn more and experiment with more HTML over time.

The codes in the table below are the codes I shall be explaining in more detail over the next few pages. Don't worry too much about them all at once, just take things slowly to start with.

Table 14: Basic HTML codes

HTML code	Description
`<p>`	Inserts a paragraph break between pictures or text
` `	Moves your text or pictures to the next line
`<center>`	Places your picture or text in the centre of the page
`</center>`	Stops placing text or pictures in the centre
`<font>`	Used with other instructions, this code will alter the appearance of your text
`</font>`	Stops the change you made to the text
`<font color="red">`	Changes all the words that follow to red until </font> stops doing it
`<font size="5">`	Makes your text larger or small depending upon the number entered, it will stay at that size until </font> is entered
`<img src=" ">`	This code will make an image appear on your page (it needs a web address of the picture between the quote marks to work)
`<a href=" "> </a>`	This pair of codes when used with the address of another web page will create a live 'clickable' link

There are a number of other codes which alter the size of pictures and colours; these are used in conjunction with the codes opposite.

These codes will need to be added to your auctions via the 'enter your own HTML' section of the 'Title and Description' page when

 The codes can be either upper or lower case.

listing your item. It may prove easier at the beginning to clear all of the existing code from your page, enter a few codes, and then revert back to the 'standard entry' method to complete your auctions in the traditional way.

Most of the codes I will show below work in pairs, a bit like a light switch: one code turns the function on and then a second code will turn it off again. The codes are all contained within angle brackets < and >. The code to turn off a function is a forward slash /. Therefore, the code to centre an item or picture is <center> and to turn off the function we would use </center>.

Note the American spelling of center!

Background colour

The first thing we shall do is change the background colour of the auction page. Due to the construction of the eBay auction pages, the code used may seem a little strange if you are familiar with HTML. Try it out and see how you get on.

At the top of your page type this code:

```
<table height="100%" width="100%" bgcolor="Blue">
<tbody>
<tr>
<td>
```

Your description and pictures would fit in here

```
</td>
</tr>
</tbody>
</table>
```

These few lines will colour your page blue. To make your background yellow, just replace 'blue' with 'yellow' in the code, and so on. (Note that the word color has no letter u!)

Outside border

In place of the listing designer offered by eBay, you can create your own border by using some HTML code and save yourself some money. The most basic type of design would just be a single colour around your description. The code below will create that effect and produce a blue border around a yellow background. To practice with this, just delete all the existing code and copy all the following into the page.

```
<center>
<table height="100%" cellpadding="15" width="100%"
bgcolor="blue">
<tbody>
<tr>
<td>
<table height="100%" width="100%" bgcolor="yellow">
<tbody>
<tr>
<td>
<center>
```

Your description and pictures would fit in here

```
</center>
</td>
</tr>
</tbody>
</table>
</td>
</tr>
</tbody>
</table>
</center>
```

As before, to change the colour of the border, just replace 'blue' with another colour. To make the border wider, change the number after the word 'cellpadding'; a larger number will make the border wider.

Patterned outside border

To replace the single colour border with a patterned design of your own will require a link to the original image. Instead of telling the browser what colour it should be, we will instead refer it to a file stored somewhere on the internet, maybe as a .jpg file on your free picture hosting site.

The procedure is much the same as above, but this time the words 'bgcolor=blue' are replaced with background="http://the address of your image.jpg" The code for the template would now read:

```
<center>
<table height="100%" cellpadding="15" width="100%"
background="http://the address of your image.jpg">
<tbody>
<tr>
<td>
<table height="100%" width="100%" bgcolor="yellow">
<tbody>
<tr>
<td>
<center>
<p>
```

Your description and pictures would fit in here

```
</center>
</td>
</tr>
</tbody>
</table>
</td>
</tr>
</tbody>
</table>
</center>
```

By changing the image that you link to, you will be able to create almost any type of border.

Once you have settled on the style of border and colour of background, you can revert back to the standard method of entering your description and the design template you have created will remain and can be used in all of your future auctions.

There are a number of other functions that you can perform using HTML code. This is by no means an exhaustive list.

Loading external pictures directly into your description

Using the piece of code that we looked at in the previous section:

```
<img src="http:// the address of your picture is in
here.jpg">
```

We can now copy this directly into the HTML page and load in as many pictures as we wish. Your auction design would now look like this:

```
<center>
<table height="100%" cellpadding="15" width="100%"
background="http://thebackgroundimageURL.jpg">
<tbody>
<tr>
<td>
<table height="100%" width="100%" bgcolor="yellow">
<tbody>
<tr>
<td>
<center>
<p>
```

Your description would fit in here and the pictures below

```
</center>
<p>
<img src="http://the address of your picture is in
here.jpg">
<p>
<img src="http://the address of your picture is in
here.jpg">
<p>
<img src="http://the address of your picture is in
here.jpg">
<p>
</td>
</tr>
</tbody>
</table>
</td>
</tr>
</tbody>
</table>
</center>
```

In the above example, I have chosen to load three pictures into the auction, placed them one above the other, separated them with a single line '<p>', and centred them on the page by using '<center>'.

When viewed, your auction will now display the pictures as they were loaded onto your hosting service. If they were not edited before saving to the internet, they could be huge as there is no restriction on the size of these pictures. Earlier in the book, we looked at the preferred size for a picture, ideally one that would avoid a lower scroll bar on the screen – a picture size of 640 x 480 pixels would achieve this. You can either edit the pictures before you load them onto your hosting site, or alter the size within your code by using 'height' and 'width' codes. The instruction to load your pictures would then look something like this:

```
<img height="480" width="640" src="http://the address of
your picture is in here.jpg">
<p>
<img height="400" width="300" src="http://the address of
your picture is in here.jpg">
<p>
<img height="200" width="300" src="http://the address of
your picture is in here.jpg">
<p>
```

Each picture would now be a different size, just select the best option for you. The numbers represent how many pixels high or wide your picture is.

TIP   Beware of using the same height and width rules for both landscape and portrait pictures, one of them will look very strange.

Cross-sell your other auctions

We have already looked at some ways of making your visitors aware of your other auctions. Now we can place direct links to these auctions using HTML. The first step is to include a link in the form of a word within a sentence, that when clicked will load your other auction. We can use the same code as before when we were using inserts to link to the eBay home page. To re-cap:

```
<a href="http://ebay.co.uk/">eBay home page</a>
```

This time we will replace the 'ebay.co.uk' with the address of the auction we want to link to and change the words 'eBay home page' to better describe the auction. It could look something like this:

```
Thanks for visiting our auction, please also check our <a
href="http://address of the auction you want to show">other
great item</a>
```

If the visitor wants to see the other great item, they just click on the words and it will appear.

To get the address of the destination auction, you will need to open a second browser and display the auction you want. At the top of the page is the address line, highlight the whole line and copy it. Now paste the line into the sentence above between the quotes. The code will then look something like:

```
Thanks for visiting our auction, please also check our <a
href="http://cgi.ebay.co.uk/ws/eBayISAPI.dll?ViewItem&item=
601023843592">other great item</a>
```

(As you can see, it is well worth learning how to copy and paste text, as you don't want to manually type code like the above!)

Practice this process a few times and it should work for you. To link to more than one auction, just copy the code and change the address and 'clickable' words.

Adding small pictures to your links

To move things on one stage further, consider the use of a small picture of the item that you wish your visitors to click through to. Not only will you be able to tell them about it, but now they can see it. The HTML code builds on the previous idea and will now include a link to the picture of the item as well.

The code will look like this;

```
Thanks for visiting our auction, please also check our <a
href="http://address of the auction you want to show"><img
src="http://address of the picture.jpg">other great
item</a>.
```

Use the picture that has already been loaded onto eBay for the destination auction. In your second browser, view the auction and right click over the small picture at the top of the listing, now click 'properties'. Here you will find the address (or URL), just copy this line and paste it into the code above.

In summary, to use a picture link to your other auctions, you will need both the address of the auction, and the address of the picture within that auction. Without any further action, the picture of your destination auction will appear very large within your description, so we will need to alter the height and width again just as we did when loading in our main pictures. As a default, your picture links will show a border, this can be removed by using 'border=0'. I will add this below.

If you choose, you could have a key message appear when a mouse curser hovers over one of your pictures, it will appear for a while and then disappear. The example overleaf shows how to add the message 'we are always happy to combine lots and reduce postage'.

A full HTML template might end up looking something like the one overleaf.

Sample HTML code for a listing page

```
<center>
<table height="100%" cellpadding="15" width="100%"
background="http://address of your chosen border image.jpg">
<tbody>
<tr>
<td>
<table height="100%" width="100%" bgcolor="yellow">
<tbody>
<tr>
<td>
<center>
<br><font size="5" color="red">The Title of your Listing
</font>
<p>Your description could be written at the top and the
pictures displayed below, or swap them around if you so
wish.
<p>Use this space to fully describe your item, in this
instance it's a selection of Playmobil.
<p>Use text of different <font color="green">colours
</font>and <font size="6">sizes</font>.
<p>Convince the visitor that they should bid on your item.
<p>
<center><img src="http://address of your photobucket
picture.jpg" height="480" width="640"></center>
<p>
<center>
Thanks for visiting our auction, please visit us again, we
always have new things available.
<p>
Please also check our <a href="http://address of the auction
you want to show"><img height="40" width="50"
src="http://address of the picture.jpg" border="0" alt="We
are always happy to combine lots & reduce shipping">
Playmobil</a>
and
<a href="http://address of the auction you want to show">
<img height="50" width="40" src="http://address of the
picture.jpg" alt="We are always happy to combine lots &
reduce shipping">Lego airport</a>.
<p>
</center>
</td>
</tr>
</tbody>
</table>
</td>
</tr>
</tbody>
</table>
</center>
```

This would appear in your eBay listing as shown below.

Fig 16. Screenshot of sample page

In this example I have chosen a mottled blue pattern for the border, a yellow centre space and have changed the size and colour of some words. I have included one picture, but to include more, just repeat the code to load a picture. The two small pictures at the bottom of the page are live links, they will take the visitor directly to the auction for the item shown.

The line alt–"We are always happy to combine lots & reduce shipping" means this phrase will be shown when a curser is placed over the picture.

This is only a snapshot of practical HTML codes that can be used. For more codes and advice on where to use them, sign up for my free weekly newsletter at www.ebaybulletin.co.uk (details are at the back of this book).

The great news is that all these additional elements of your auction do not cost any more in fees.

By using these techniques in only a handful of auctions, you will soon recover the cost of this book!

This section has only just touched on the power of HTML to increase the success of your eBay auctions. There is not enough space to demonstrate all the possibilities, just experiment and you will see that almost anything is possible.

Top five tips for the use of HTML

1. **Be aware of page load times**
   The more elements you have within your auction, the longer pages take to load – don't get too carried away.

2. **Use moving text and distracting animations only in moderation**
   I did not expand on moving text or animations; they can work very well, but could also distract the bidders from your actual auction.

3. **Use plain background colours**
   Make your auction easy to read. Simple, bright colours work best.

4. **Make use of external links**
   Externals links are great, they remove the clutter and allow you to add value to your description in many ways.

5. **Use large pictures within the description**
   Large pictures sell items, make use of them, they really work.

Summary

You should now:

- be proficient in the basic computer techniques of **copy'n'pasting** and opening **multiple browser windows**;

- understand how to use **inserts**, including creating links to external web pages and pictures;

- know how to include **extra pictures** in your item listing; and

- know how to use basic **HTML** to enhance the look of your auction pages.

You've come a long way! You now know how to list items on eBay and how to make your item pages attractive and sophisticated, such that they will be better than 95% of the competition. However, don't get too confident just yet. There's an important chapter coming up next – on fraud!

Fraud on eBay

Overview

In any environment where money changes hands, there is the potential for fraud. eBay is no exception to this rule. There is fraud on the site and it can be costly if you get caught. Knowing what to look for and applying a little caution in your eBay dealings should significantly limit your chances of becoming a victim of fraud.

There is an old saying that if something seems too good to be true, then it probably is. This is as true on eBay as anywhere. Beware of the auction that claims to have a genuine article for sale at a tenth of the retail price – you may well end up with something not quite as you expected.

There are several areas of potential fraud within eBay: sellers may try to relieve you of your money under false pretences, buyers can purchase items and then default on payment, and even your eBay or PayPal account details can be stolen.

This chapter is about some of the fraudulent techniques that I am aware of, along with a few examples of what to look out for. It is by no means a comprehensive list as the fraudsters are coming up with new scams all the time.

Just how big a target you will be as a seller on eBay will be decided by the kind of items you sell and their value. High value, negotiable items, such as mobile phones or computers are more likely to be a target than your rare Val Doonican LPs.

> The items I sell have an average sale price of just £10, so my experience of being defrauded by buyers is limited. If I were to sell higher value items, I am sure that it would increase.

Types of fraud

The areas of potential fraud we will look at are:

1. Payment fraud

2. Postage fraud

3. eBay account hijack

4. PayPal account hijack

These are explained below.

1. Payment fraud

Receiving a payment for an item is great, the reward for all your hard work. However there is always a concern that the payment may not be good; perhaps the cheque will bounce or the electronic payment may be retracted. This is more of a concern for international sales and for items with a high value.

The majority of payments will be fine. There are, however, a few simple precautions to follow which should ensure a trouble free completion to your trade.

1. **Do not sell your item outside of the eBay process**
    It is possible to end an auction early and sell to the highest bidder, or place a new 'buy it now' listing for a pre-determined price. Selling items outside of the process will remove any seller's protection that may apply, and of course you will not be eligible for feedback.

2. **Check the winning bidder's details**
    Are you happy with their feedback comments, if they have any? Check the member's contact information against the postal address provided by the buyer. If anything does not appear to be correct, don't send the item and contact eBay with your concerns.

3. **Is the trade covered by any fraud or seller protection?**
    If the payment has been received electronically, check the service being used and see if the trade is covered by a protection policy. If there is such a policy, ensure that you comply with the terms of this cover. The most

common problem that I am aware of is where the buyer asks for the item to be shipped to an 'unconfirmed' address, which nullifies the seller protection clause. This will be more of a concern for higher priced or popular items.

4. **Ensure that payment clears before sending the item**
Standard cheques can be presented to your bank, and e-cheques work in the same way: after a few days, they are cleared. If the buyer is paying with a credit card, you can contact the credit card company if in any doubt and confirm the identity of the buyer.

> I choose not to accept credit cards directly, only via PayPal.

Use good judgement when accepting a cheque or money order as payment for a high value item. Before posting the item, check with your bank to ensure that the payment method is valid, and that funds have cleared and are available. If you have reason to believe that the buyer paid, or is attempting to pay, with fraudulent funds, contact eBay so that they can investigate and take appropriate action.

In the event that the buyer sends payment that is found to be fraudulent, contact the police in your area and the area where the buyer resides. eBay will fully cooperate with all such inquiries. If payment is reversed, stopped, or cannot be received, you should also contact the payment issuer (credit card company, issuing bank, PayPal, etc.) to review the options available to you.

If you have already sent the item and have been unable to receive payment, please review the 'Defrauded Sellers' page on eBay for other options you can pursue.

If you are unable to receive payment, you may also be able to request a Final Value Fee credit by filing a claim under the Unpaid Item process.

> I have had only two examples of defaulted payment since trading; both were bounced cheques for small amounts where unfortunately I had already dispatched the items.

Five areas of extra caution for a seller

1. **International payment**
   International payments are likely to be received via PayPal or similar companies, and could also include e-checks. If you do take overseas personal cheques, remember that they take a lot longer to clear.

2. **Revised shipping information**
   If you are asked to ship your item to an address other than a verified one shown on the PayPal documentation, be wary, as you will fall outside of the 'Standard Purchase Protection Program'.

3. **Unknown or new buyers**
   New bidders will not have a track record with eBay. If selling a high value item, check their contact information and maybe even give them a call before sending the item.

4. **Unusual bidding activity**
   If your item reaches a level that you didn't expect, you are either very lucky or there may be a problem when the auction ends. Check the bidding history of the highest two bidders using the advanced search and see if they have been active in the same auctions before. If in any doubt, ask for more information from them.

5. **Orders shipped 'rush' or 'overnight'**
   Be cautious if you are asked to ship the item in a hurry, a birthday is the favourite request. Let the payment clear first and if PayPal was used, only ship to the confirmed address.

2. Postage fraud

eBay encourages buyers and sellers to resolve any issues involving shipping by communicating directly with each other. If you have a question about excessive shipping and handling charges, refer to the Excessive Postage/Handling help page for more information.

If an item was lost or damaged in the post, you can request contact information from eBay and call your trading partner to explain the situation and work out a solution. You should also consider contacting the postal service for assistance. If you send a notification of shipment when you send the item, your buyer will be expecting it and should contact you if it doesn't arrive in a reasonable time.

It is very difficult to prove if an item did arrive and the buyer is just claiming that it didn't – especially if the buyer is overseas. For higher value items, ask the buyer to pay for insurance.

Items that are lost or damaged in the post are not covered under the eBay Standard Purchase Protection Program unless you are the *buyer* and one of the following conditions apply:

- You purchased postage insurance and the seller failed to insure the item.

- You purchased postage insurance and you or the seller filed a claim with the postal service, but the claim was denied due to poor packaging.

- You purchased postage insurance and you or the seller filed a claim with the postal service and they awarded the seller reimbursement but the seller failed to send a refund to you.

If one or more of these conditions apply and you are still unable to resolve the transaction, the buyer can use the eBay Standard Purchase Protection Program and consider opening a dispute.

Five things to ensure when shipping

1. **Obtain 'proof of postage'**

   It is free and will offer some protection against items that are claimed to be lost. The proof of postage will of course also show that you did send the item.

2. **Insist on insurance for high value items**

   For higher value items, add insurance to your shipping requirements. This will be a relatively small amount in comparison to the value of the item.

3. **Ship to confirmed addresses**

   It is such an important point that it needs to be mentioned again: with higher value items, only ship to the confirmed address.

4. **Include a return address**

   Add a return address on the back of each parcel; there is always a chance that it might find its way back to you.

5. **Contact buyer when sent**

   As soon as you dispatch the item, notify the buyer. It is great for customer care and will advise them when to expect it.

---

3. eBay account hijack

One of the most popular pastimes of fraudsters is trying to gain access to your eBay account. They will do this by sending spoof emails to you in many different formats, each designed to have you enter your eBay ID and password onto a website that you accessed via the email.

These emails could claim that you have been invited to become a Power Seller, or that your account details are incorrect. They may warn you that if you do not verify your details immediately, your account will be suspended. The list of inventive excuses is growing longer every week.

The best spoof I have seen lately is an email which is a very good copy of the 'Question for sellers' email. It asks when an item is to be posted and, as with the question for seller email, there is a link supposedly to the eBay item. You will be curious to know which item it was for and will click on the link. A page will then ask for your eBay ID and password, which you will enter as you are used to this and the fraudster will have your details.

All of these deceptions have one goal: to take temporary control of your eBay account.

Once they have control, your password will be changed, locking you out of your own account and while eBay investigate the situation, a number of things will happen. Firstly, the account ID into which you receive electronic payments (this is usually your email address) will be changed. A number of high value items will be placed under your account, these will be very popular items offered with a 'Buy It Now' option well below the average price for the item. They will stipulate that only electronic payment can be used to buy them.

Any potential bargain hunters will find the items, they may even check your feedback, which will be very good, and they may decide to purchase. When they pay, the money will be transferred to a different account and of course no item will be dispatched. You have been used to exploit the bidder, who will lose their money.

4. PayPal account hijack

A similar process is used to try and gain control of your PayPal account. As a result, this time it is the seller that needs to take care. Many emails are sent asking you to verify your PayPal details, or warning you that an unauthorised change has been made. The goal is the same as before: to take control of your account.

Once the fraudster has an account, they will bid in pairs on a higher value item, such as a mobile phone. The bid will be raised much higher than the value of the item and when the auction ends, payment will be made and you will be asked to send the item to a different address than that shown on the

PayPal documentation. Having achieved a much higher price than you expected, you may well agree and post the item once the funds have been received in your account.

When the PayPal account is restored back to its correct owner, the payment will be recovered from the seller and placed back in the PayPal account, leaving the seller with no money and no item.

I have included a selection of spoof emails within this book that should illustrate what to look for.

What eBay will and won't do concerning fraud

eBay have an interest to make the site as free from fraud as possible, as the threat of being defrauded will deter some people from trading. The scale of the site makes policing every trade impossible, there is just too much happening at any one time.

eBay provides the venue for buyers and sellers to come together and trade. They can take action against members who break the rules, but they do rely on the wider community reporting such activity. eBay state that their goal is;

"To create a safe trading environment for our members by facilitating communication and providing services to protect against fraud."

This means that they will lay down the rules and take action if they are broken.

What eBay does

When suspicious activity is reported to eBay, they will investigate the circumstances and then either warn or suspend accounts that are found to violate eBay policies.

eBay provide the framework and systems that allow buyers and sellers to obtain contact information from each other. Before a trade is completed, it is possible to find out a considerable amount of information on a member; and following the completion of a trade, more personal information is made available.

eBay works closely with PayPal to help buyers and sellers resolve their transaction problems. For items paid for with PayPal, members may file a complaint through PayPal's 'Buyer Complaint Process'. For all other items, eBay provide the 'Item Not Received' or 'Significantly Not as Described' process.

eBay offer a purchase protection scheme and PayPal Buyer Protection offers up to £500 in free coverage for qualified items paid for via PayPal. For most other items, eBay's Standard Purchase Protection programme provides reimbursement to buyers up to £120 (less £15 to cover processing costs) for loss from non-delivery or misrepresentation.

What eBay does not do

eBay are unable to take action on a member's behalf. This includes contacting a member directly to ask about the status of an item. They will provide contact information, but will not become directly involved in the dispute.

Since eBay are not involved in the actual transaction, they cannot force a member to live up to their obligation. This also includes pursuing any action outside of the eBay community, which will be up to the individual member to follow.

What to do if you have been defrauded

eBay urges buyers and sellers to use both email and the telephone to contact one another to resolve any issues that may arise. You can get the phone number for your trading partner by going to 'Find Contact Information' under 'Advanced Search'. Most issues can be resolved through direct communication between buyers and sellers, quite often it is just a misunderstanding.

If efforts to communicate directly with your buyer or seller are unsuccessful, consider the following:

- Contact PayPal if this method of payment was used. You may be covered for up to £500 by PayPal Buyer Protection.

- If you did not pay through PayPal, contact your credit card company or payment issuer. Credit card issuers typically provide protection in instances of online fraud. Contact your credit card company to learn about what type of coverage and terms they provide.

- Use eBay's 'Item Not Received' or 'Significantly Not as Described' dispute process.

- Through this dispute process, trading partners are able to communicate online to resolve transaction problems. If problems cannot be resolved, buyers may then submit an eBay 'Standard Purchase Protection claim'. eBay also reviews Item Not Received or Significantly Not as Described disputes for possible violations of the Seller Non-performance policy.

- Contact the police. To find the contact details for your local police force go to: www.police.uk

Summary

You should now:

- understand the types of fraud that exist on eBay;

- know what eBay will and will not do; and

- know what to do if you've been the subject of fraud.

Not a pleasant topic, fraud, but it has to be dealt with. Back to a more attractive topic in the next chapter – how to develop your business to make more money.

Developing your online business

Overview

As your experience of eBay grows, along with your ability to manage all aspects of your business, you may decide to move up to the next level. This may involve dedicating more time to your enterprise, which should result in more rewards. eBay is completely flexible: if you are content with a certain income and workload, remain at that level; if on the other hand you would like to develop your business, there are a few areas which could be considered.

The ideas that I will mention here are my thoughts on a possible way forward. How you actually grow your enterprise will depend on many things, but these should stimulate a few ideas.

Building on your brand

Now you have successfully traded on eBay, even just once, you have the beginnings of a brand — a name that customers will associate with certain levels of service and product quality. If the buying experience was a good one, your customers may well return to see if you have other items of interest. It is possible to use this goodwill to drive as many visits to your auctions as possible. This section looks at some of the options that will help to build your business reputation and give some ideas on how to encourage customers to return to your site. The ultimate goal must be to ensure that each time the individual visits eBay, they will visit your auctions.

eBay Shops

Opening an eBay Shop could be the next step for your online business. They operate in much the same way as ordinary auctions, but there are quite a few advantages if you are selling the same item again and again.

eBay have created a number of tools specifically for the shop owner. These will enable you to develop your eBay brand and should encourage buyers to buy more products.

These management tools include:

- **Customisation** – have complete control over the look and feel of your shop (colours, graphics, content, etc.)

- The ability to list your items in a special **Shop Inventory format** which has lower fees and longer active durations.

- Organise and display your items with your own **custom categories**.

- **Keyword searches within your Shop**, which buyers can use to find goods.

- Control the cross-promotion of your other items when buyers view, bid on, or win an item.

- A **unique internet web address** (URL) that you can promote to your buyers. This address will appear on external search engines, driving potential customers directly to your shop.

- **Sales and visitor traffic reports** to let you know how successful your Shop is.

There are some criteria to meet before you can open a Shop; currently these are:

1. You must have PayPal stated as a payment method, *plus* minimum feedback rating of 5.
   or
   no PayPal account, but a minimum feedback rating of 10.

2. You must have an automatic payment method selected to pay your fees to eBay.

Three formats of eBay Shop

There are three formats for an eBay Shop:

1. Basic

2. Featured

3. Anchor

These are explained below.

Basic

Fig 17. Screenshot of a Basic Shop listing

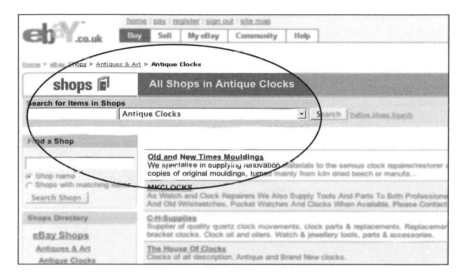

With a Basic Shop subscription, you can automatically·

- Showcase all your listings in your shop front.

- Drive buyers to your custom URL.

- List in Shop Inventory format for only £0.03/30 days.

- Use Merchandising Manager to cross-sell your inventory on your bid and checkout pages.

- Receive monthly performance reports on all your eBay sales.

Featured

Fig 18 and 19. Screenshots of a Featured Shop listing

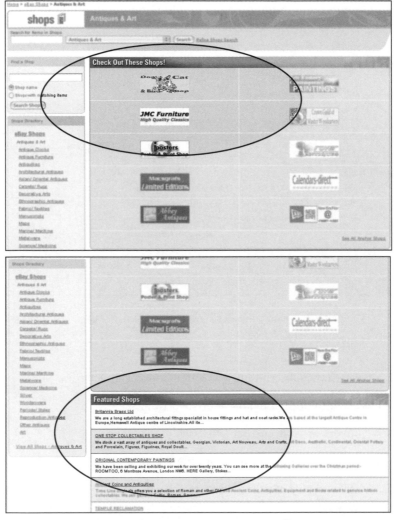

With a Featured Shop, you get all the Basic Shop benefits, plus:

- cross-selling of your Shop inventory on all your listings pages.

- priority placement in 'Related Shops' sections.

- featured placement on the eBay Shops home page.

- prime Positioning in the top level directory pages where you have items listed.

Anchor

Fig 20 and 21. Screenshots of an Anchor Shop listing

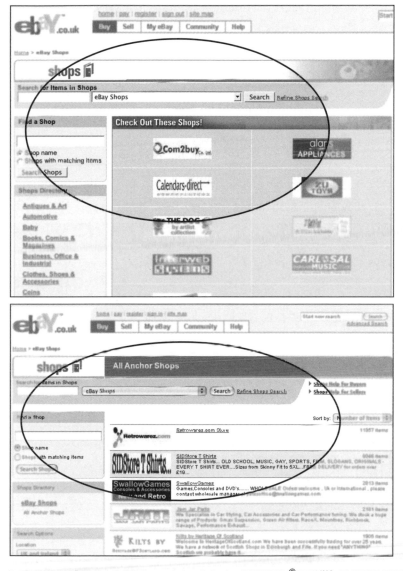

With an Anchor Shop, you get all the Basic and Featured Shop benefits, plus:

- Showcase placement of your logo within the eBay Shops Directory pages.
- Premium placement in 'Related Shops' sections of the Search and Browse pages.

eBay shop fee structure

To open an eBay Shop you pay a monthly subscription fee. Each item you list in your eBay Shop incurs an insertion fee and, if it sells, a final value fee. The subscription fees are as follows:

Table 15: eBay Shop subscription fees

Shop format	Fee
Basic	£6/month
Featured	£30/month
Anchor	£300/month

Table 16: eBay Shop insertion fees

Duration	Insertion fee	Surcharge	Total
30 days	£0.03	N/A	£0.03
90 days	£0.03	£0.10	£0.13
Good until cancelled*	£0.03/30 days	N/A	£0.03/30 days

Note: The insertion fee covers any quantity.

*Good until cancelled listings are recurring 30 day listings. eBay will charge the relevant fees every 30 days.

> At this point I do not have an eBay Shop, as most of the items I sell are all different. I just never took the plunge. As I am now including more fixed price items to supplement my regular auctions, it is something I shall be doing in the near future.

eBay Shops are certainly suited for sellers who stock repeat items. The 'Good until cancelled' option means that one listing can run for months, significantly reducing admin time. Sellers with large numbers of items for sale at any one time can also make good use of Shops as they have the facility for buyers to perform key word searches within the Shop.

You can browse all the Shops on eBay, just the same way as you would by visiting a traditional shopping mall. Shops are listed in a directory in the same way that the main categories are structured, so you can browse through similar Shops if you are looking for a particular item.

There are thousands of Shops on eBay – the last time I checked the total was 35,450 with 5,100 in the automotive area alone. Shops can be displayed by their name in alphabetical order or by the number of items they stock. In November 2005, the range of items was between 46,937 in the most populated Shop and one item in the least populated Shop.

Seller tools

It is in eBay's interest for sellers to be able to run more auctions and sell more products; they will, of course, make more money from fees. To assist the seller with some of the less interesting tasks, eBay have developed a number of *Seller Tools*. There are still some older tools in use and there will undoubtedly be more released in the coming months. At this time there are three tools which might be of interest and worthy of a little more detail:

1. Selling Manager
2. Selling Manager Pro
3. Turbo Lister

These are explained below.

1. Selling Manager

Selling Manager is a management tool that will assist with most tasks from scheduling your listings to managing your sales; it even helps print address labels. This tool will work within your 'My eBay' section and is compatible with all other eBay tools, such as the standard 'sell your item' form which we looked at earlier.

Selling Manager will provide an immediate estimate of your total sales and switch back to the original 'My eBay' format at any time. This service is currently free of charge; just visit the 'seller tools' from the site map and upgrade online.

The facilities offered by Selling Manager are as follows:

Management tools

- Preview, edit, reschedule or cancel scheduled listings online.

- Monitor your active listings in real time.

- Up to date summary of the number of pending active and sold listings you have.

- Track your gross sales amount for active and sold listings.

After the auction ends

- Find out when your listings end real time and track your unsold items.

- Bulk re-list your sold and unsold items.

- Keep track of your buyer communication and whether your items have been paid or shipped.

- Store sales and customer information.

- Use seven fully customisable email templates to communicate with your buyers.

- Record your buyer communication to help with Non-Paying Buyers (NPBs).

- Store up to 10 custom feedback messages to re-use.

- Keep track of whether your buyer has left you a positive, negative or neutral feedback.

- Print shipping labels.

- Print invoices.

- Monthly view of archived sales.

2. Selling Manager Pro

As you have come to expect, eBay also offer an upgrade to the Selling Manager service – *Selling Manager Pro*. This service is free for the first 30 days on a trial basis and then costs £4.99 per month.

This tool has been created for the high volume seller and small business. It will allow for bulk listings and builds on the Selling Manager management tools.

The additional facilities include:

- **Inventory management**
  Manage your auctions and shop items by keeping track of your inventory. It is not good to have stock in storage that you don't know about. It is also not good to sell an item and then realise that you don't have any left. You can also re-list your items in bulk.

- **Listing statistics**
  Understand the success of your product and see which items sell best by calculating your average selling price.

- **Listing, emailing, sending feedback and printing invoices in bulk**
  Selling Manager Pro will perform most of your mundane tasks in bulk.

- **Automatic email and feedback**
  Automatic completion of feedback and email generation.

- **Profit and loss reports**
  With monthly profit and loss reports, you will be able to stay better informed about how your business and the market in general is performing. These reports include your eBay fees.

> The 6p fee to schedule in advance is removed when you subscribe to Selling Manager Pro, so if you schedule enough items, it could be worth it for that alone.

3. Turbo Lister

Listing auctions can be very time consuming, especially if you have to write out the description each time. eBay have thought of this and introduced a tool called *Turbo Lister*. As the name suggests, this is a very fast way of loading hundreds or even thousands of items onto eBay in one go.

With this tool, you will be able to create your listings on your computer and then upload them to eBay in one hit. It has been designed for medium to high volume sellers and is currently free to use. Some of the main attractions of Turbo Lister are:

- It contains a **design editor** which will help create a more professional listing and you don't need to know any HTML.

- You can load **multiple items** once and save the details for use in the future, which saves writing them out again.

- You can add pictures to the listings without being connected to the internet. This might save some money if you are on a 'pay as you go' network connection.

- You can insert notes on payment terms, shipping details and any other messages that you would normally include.

TIP As Turbo Lister is free, try it and see how you get on. Some sellers just don't like it, but you won't know unless you try.

Seller tool fees

Table 17: eBay Seller tool fees

Listing tool	Fee
Selling Manager	Free
Selling Manager Pro	£4.99 per month
Turbo Lister	Free

Encourage repeat sales

Once established, your site will attract repeat visits as regular customers check back to see what you have for sale. Increasing and maintaining this customer loyalty will result in higher bids and ultimately higher profits.

There are several things that can be done to increase this return rate – they are all based around the customer experience.

- **Hold items**

  Be prepared to hold items while customers continue to shop at your site. Offer a discount on postage for multiple purchases.

- **List regularly**

  Keep your site well stocked with items. Customers may return a couple of times, but if they do not see any items for sale, they may not return again.

- **Sell similar items over a number of days**

  If you are selling a collection of items, list the items over a number of days. Mention that you will have more of the same tomorrow and bidders will return each day to see what is new. Make sure that you cross-sell other items that might also be of interest.

- **Specialise**

  If you specialise in one particular line, you will establish a regular customer base. If ever they need that certain item, they will visit you to see what is available. Use additional IDs for different types of item.

Create a USP for your business

A Unique Selling Point, or USP, is just a smart way of saying that you need to differentiate your business from the competition. Go one step further in some areas and stand out from the crowd. Buyers will visit you again because of that little extra you offer, they may also mention it in their feedback comment, which can only help.

- **Speed of dispatch**

  Quick dispatch of items will certainly improve your repeat business. Once an item has been won and paid for, the buyer wants it the very next day. Don't promise what cannot be delivered, but send the items as quick as you can; it also gets them out of the way and saves on storage space.

- **Returns policy**

  Develop a simple, no quibble, returns policy. Be wary of the bidder who buys to try and then returns. Experience will show the best returns policy for your line of business. If a bidder can buy knowing that the item can be returned under certain circumstances, they will have more confidence in you as a seller.

- **Customer service**

  Send an acknowledgement email following receipt of payment and again on dispatch of goods. Include a note in each parcel to close the trade and invite the buyer back to your site.

  TIP Using HTML, design an email signature that carries a link to your eBay site.

- **Quality of packing**

  This has been mentioned many times already, but it is one of the big areas where you can impress your buyer. Good packing will entice them to return again, knowing that great care will be taken with their items.

I have settled on three areas of my business where I try to excel. I aim to achieve them with every trade, they are:

1. Quality of packing

2. Speed of delivery

3. Communications throughout the transaction

Once you have established your operating processes, it will become second nature to pack in a certain way, or send emails at certain stages of the trade. My feedback comments are full of references to these three areas – it really works.

TIP When you have decided on your key areas, write them in your item listings; tell your bidders what you will do, above and beyond what they might expect.

Why feedback is so important

Feedback is perhaps the main reason that eBay has become so successful. Without it, how would you know that the seller will do what they say? On the strength of a feedback score, we will send money to a complete stranger – possibly in a different country – in the hope and expectation that they will send us some goods. It is very powerful!

Maintaining a high feedback score is very difficult. It is extremely hard to please everybody all of the time and negative feedbacks will happen, it is only to be expected if you have been trading for some time.

Feedback as a sales tool

We have already discussed how positive feedback can be obtained by really pleasing your customer and this will work in your favour to stimulate further sales. How you leave your feedback for buyers will also count towards your sales. In the first place, always leave feedback for your buyers. For many new members, feedback is vital and if they suspect that you may not leave feedback, they may be deterred from bidding. How you actually leave feedback is also something to be considered. Choose the words you use so that the buyer feels special, it may just prompt them to return again.

Coping with negative feedback

You are quite likely to receive a negative feedback, or even more than one. You may choose to respond to the feedback. If so, rather than being aggressive in your response, make a point to all those who may read the comment at a later date; reassure anybody reading it that the negative was a one off, just a mistake and not something to worry about. If you are rude in your response, it may make the situation worse.

No matter how many positive feedbacks you earn, bidders will always seek out the negative ones, just out of curiosity.

> I currently have two negative feedbacks in over 6,000 trades. It hurt the first time, but does not seem to impact on my trading activity.

Extending your customer relationship

Once you have traded successfully with your buyer, you will have started a relationship with them and it is possible to nurture this and hopefully turn them into a loyal customer. It is important not to send any unsolicited emails as this is treated as spam. There are, however, a couple of things that you may like to try:

1. **Permission based campaigns**

   On your dispatch email, consider a line which says something like, 'If you would like details of all our forthcoming auctions, please let us know and we will send you a regular update'. If the buyer responds, you have their permission to send them emails in the future. What you include in these emails is up to you, but you should find that it will stimulate interest in your auctions.

2. **Newsletter**

   You may consider a customer newsletter. This could contain hints and tips on eBay, links to help sites, anything really. It could also contain 'Affiliate sales links' which I will discuss in the next few pages.

Securing more stock

The most closely guarded secret of all salespeople is where they obtain their stock. Nobody who trades on eBay, or anywhere else, will advise of their stock supplier. If you manufacture your own items, or have an existing supplier relationship, then stick with what you know. If you do not have such an arrangement, this section may give some insight into a few areas that might just lead to a source of goods to sell.

Possible sources are:

1. Traditional wholesalers

2. eBay

3. Other auction sites

4. Traditional auctions

5. Second-hand items

6. Retail outlets

These are explained below.

1. Traditional wholesalers

If you know the kind of thing that you would like to sell, you should be able to find a wholesaler who can supply the items. Check your local press, Yellow Pages and the internet. It is possible to buy lists of wholesalers that have been compiled by a third party. For a few pounds, this option may save you time trawling through the internet.

Ensure that the margins on these goods is high enough, and be prepared to buy in bulk. Anticipate the storage issues and impact on your cash flow.

2. eBay

eBay is a great place to buy goods for resale. Once you have mastered all the elements of this book, you will understand for your own area what sells and for what price. Check eBay for sellers who do not know the value of their items, buy them cheaply and resell them in a more professional way.

Look for sellers who:

- **Trade only with the UK**
  These sellers have severely restricted their market place, and their items will not reach high sale prices.

- **Do not accept PayPal**
  Sellers who do not accept PayPal will again restrict their customer base. Even if they sell worldwide, overseas bidders will find it difficult to pay. (When your search results are shown on the screen, sort by 'Payment: PayPal last' and the Non-PayPal items will be at the top.)

- **Accept only a few methods of payment**
  Reducing the buyers payment options will reduce prices and should allow you to pick up a bargain.

- **Have made mistakes in the description of their item**
  Maybe the spelling of a keyword is wrong; if so, fewer bidders will find the auction.

> **TIP** If you do find an item with a mistake in the title, make a small bid. Once a bid has been placed, the seller cannot revise the title, therefore locking the mistake in and restricting the number of competitors you will have for the item.

Use these techniques and you will be able to pick up stock at a reasonable price. You can then sell it on to the world, accepting many payment options, and should see an increase in value.

Sum of the parts...

Consider buying collections of items and splitting them down into more manageable lots. This will involve a higher purchase price, but the sum of the parts should be more than the entire collection, as individual items will appeal to more bidders with less money to spend.

Use the search facility as described in an earlier section and check for some of these keywords:

- Massive
- Huge
- Collection
- Lots
- Loads
- Wholesale

Remember that large collections of items will weigh a lot, these will cost more to post and are more difficult to send overseas. This is just the type of auction you should be looking for.

Buy Lego by weight, CDs by collections, mobile phone car kits and split them into component parts, trading cards by the inch and so on.

To move ahead of other eBay users using these methods to buy stock, use the advanced search facility and search for your item using:

- **Buy It Now** as a purchase option. This will allow you to obtain stock that much quicker and remove the item from circulation. Combine this search with;
- **Listings started within 1 hour** and you will be one of the first people to see the item and if it suits your needs, buy it immediately.

TIP When you find an item that looks promising, place a bid there and then. Too many times I have forgotten to check back and missed the auction end. The proxy bidding system will bid on your behalf up to your maximum amount, so just enter it once and hope no-one else finds the same auction.

Wholesale & Job Lots

There is also another great place to buy large volumes of stock on eBay – the *Wholesale* category. Access this in the same way as any other: go to the site map in the top menu and click 'Wholesale & Job Lots'. The last time I looked, there were more than 23,000 active auctions, offering everything from bulk supply of lipsticks to wholesale lots of shoes.

This is how the 23,000 entries were divided across the subcategories:

Antiques & Art (208)	Jewellery & Watches (4154)
Automotive (278)	Mixed Lots (1019)
Baby (178)	Mobile & Home Phones (859)
Books, Comics & Magazines (418)	Music (498)
Business, Office & Industrial (687)	Musical Instruments (13)
Clothes, Shoes & Accessories (3948)	Novelty Items (857)
Collectables (307)	PC & Video Gaming (216)
Computing (914)	Photography (111)
Consumer Electronics (529)	Pottery, Porcelain & Glass (95)
Crafts (383)	Sporting Goods (461)
Dolls & Bears (63)	Sports Memorabilia (36)
DVDs, Film & TV (423)	Tickets & Travel (22)
Greeting Cards/ Stationery (699)	Toys & Games (1380)
Health & Beauty (1237)	Other Wholesale & Job Lots (2449)
Home & Garden (1196)	

As you can see, there will be something here for most eBay traders.

TIP Keep the packaging that your purchases arrive in. You may well be able to re-use it for your own sales and save some money.

3. Other auction sites

eBay is not the only auction site on the internet, although it is by far the biggest. Depending on the type of items you intend to sell, you may be able to buy from one site and sell on another. Items for sale on other auction sites might not get as many visitors as eBay, so there may be a variation in prices.

Below I have listed some of the other main sites. Check them out, you never know what you might find.

- Yahoo Auctions (auctions.yahoo.com)

- Amazon Auctions (s1.amazon.com)

- UBid (www.ubid.com)

- Bidz.com (ht.bidz.com)

4. Traditional auctions

The traditional, non-cyber auction house may also be the place to obtain stock. In a traditional auction, items will usually sell to somebody in the room, so on certain days, there may not be many people present. Bid wisely, pick up a bargain, list it on eBay and sell to a global market.

5. Second-hand items

The second-hand market always has bargains to be found. Consider your local newspaper adverts, car boot sales, charity shops and so on. Once you have accumulated the knowledge of eBay and have an understanding of prices that can be obtained, you will know if a particular item could yield a profit.

When considering second-hand items for resale, there are a few things to be aware of before you make your purchase.

- Consider the **condition** with an older item. Of course, the wear and tear may be part of the item's appeal, the whole antiques market is, after all, just second-hand goods.

- Think about how much **time** will be needed to prepare the item for sale – is there just too much work involved?

Spare parts market

Used items can be a great source of spares for other models. If you are intending to sell model trains for example, then you would need a selection of spare parts. There is a market for well-priced used spares for all kinds of items, including toys, electrical items, computers and domestic appliances.

> Having recently changed our family vacuum cleaner, I was left with an old Dyson upright cleaner, still serviceable, if a little noisy. This was much too heavy for me to sell on eBay, I just don't have the packing materials. So I dismantled the machine and sold the attachments, hose, electric switches and even the power cable.

 TIP When selling replacement parts, offer them for instant purchase with 'Buy It Now'. If an item has broken, the buyer will not want to wait for a week to get the replacement part.

Second-hand items to avoid

Some things can look like a bargain, but can prove to be just too much hard work. If you do sell something that is faulty, putting it right can be costly as well as time consuming. The list below is just some of the things I would avoid when looking for used items.

- Items with **moving parts** such as videos and audio cassette tapes.

- **Computer software** which may not work on all types of computer.

- **Jigsaws** which might have parts missing.

- **Electrical items** that you cannot see working.

6. Retail outlets

It is even possible to buy stock from the high street and sell it for a profit. Old lines, discontinued stock and even sale items may well not be available overseas. Certain toys, for example, are not sold throughout the world, so a particular model in the UK may not be available elsewhere. Know your market and you will be able to make money in this way.

> In the early days of starting out on eBay, I bought Arsenal Monopoly for £24.99 in Woolworths, and then sold it on eBay the same day for £45. I enjoyed that so much, I did it six more times!

Affiliate sales

The area of affiliate sales is huge and can produce significant revenue. Many companies will pay owners of websites a commission for business that is passed to them via live links. Almost anybody with a website can apply to become an affiliate, usually through a third party who will administer the account and payments.

eBay will also pay a commission for any business passed to them from an external website. Check out Commission Junction (www.cj.com) and see if it would be of interest to you.

How it works

Affiliate schemes are managed by an intermediate company who provides all of the activity tracking for the advertiser and provides all the banners and text links that will be required. As an affiliate you will have access to these banners and text links and will be able to place them on your websites.

When a visitor to your website clicks on a banner or link, a cookie will be stored on their computer. This cookie is not harmful to your visitor, it just contains information about the affiliate.

Within the eBay Affiliate scheme, just having somebody follow a link from your site is not enough, they will have to complete an action on eBay. This could be either placing a bid on an item, buying an item through the 'Buy It Now' option or registering as a new user.

If such a transaction takes place, the cookie will capture this information and update your affiliate records, crediting you with the reward for the particular action.

It is also possible to display live auctions on your own website – as a 'virtual eBay'. This will promote your auctions and at the same time may generate extra revenue if somebody clicks and bids.

Where it can be used

Affiliate links can be used from almost any website. As you surf around the internet, you will notice links to other sites; it is quite likely that the site owner will receive a payment for passing traffic. All of the big websites use this method to raise funds and can even be rewarded on the number of page impressions that they achieve.

These links can also be used within your email signature. You could have a line that reads 'Please check out my eBay site'. This would include an HTML link as used in the previous section and incorporate your affiliate user ID. If the recipient of the email does click and then transact on eBay, you will have generated revenue by just replying to an email.

Power Seller status

As your volume of sales increases, or if the value of those sales reaches a certain level and is maintained for a period of time, you may be invited to become a *Power Seller*.

Membership to the Power Seller Program is free, and there are five levels to aspire to: Bronze, Silver, Gold, Platinum and Titanium. Each level requires a seller to meet and maintain either a pre-set level of average gross sales or a pre-set quantity of items sold for the past three months of selling activity.

The current requirements for each level are shown below.

Table 18: Power Seller qualification requirements

Power Seller level	Gross sales per month	Quantity of items sold per month
Bronze	£750	100
Silver	£1,500	300
Gold	£6,000	1,000
Platinum	£15,000	2,500
Titanium	£95,000	5,000

Membership to the Power Seller program carries advantages as shown in the table below. It also indicates to your bidders that you are serious about your eBay business and will go the extra mile to make your trades run smoothly.

Table 19: Power Seller benefits

Power Seller Level	Personal phone support	Fast priority email support	Access to dedicated Power Seller board	Invitations to eBay events
Bronze	✗	✔	✔	✔
Silver	✗	✔	✔	✔
Gold	✔	✔	✔	✔
Platinum	✔	✔	✔	✔
Titanium	✔	✔	✔	✔

How to become a Power Seller

To achieve and retain Power Seller status, you will need to:

1. Establish a track record of consistent sales achievement (see above table for minimum requirements for gross sales or quantity of items sold).

2. Maintain a minimum average monthly total of four sold listings for the past three months.

3. Be an active seller on the eBay site for a minimum duration of 90 days.

4. Achieve and maintain a minimum feedback rating of 100% and a minimum of 98% total positive feedback.

5. Be in good standing by complying with eBay Listing Policies.

6. Keep your eBay account current (i.e. no overdue payments).

7. Deliver responses to successful bidders within three business days.

8. Uphold the eBay Community Values, including honesty, timeliness and mutual respect.

I have now been a Power Seller for about 18 months and believe that it does provide my customers with the confidence that I will deliver on my promises and treat every trade, regardless of value, as they would expect. Some Power Sellers choose not to display the icon, however I do, and am very proud of it – there is a lot of hard work involved to keep it.

Trading worldwide

As your UK business continues to grow, you may well consider exporting your products both within the European Union and maybe worldwide. Each of these new markets will offer increased business opportunities, but will also require more research to manage the trade restrictions and legislation that may apply.

Whilst this book will not enter into great depth on this subject, there are a few main areas that will need to be addressed. The good news is that there are established bodies who will assist with commercial ventures outside of the UK.

Exporting to the EU

Selling your goods into Europe has fewer restrictions than exporting worldwide and there is no need for any specific customs documentation.

The EU has recently expanded and the following countries joined in May 2004: Cyprus, Czech Republic, Estonia, Hungary, Latvia, Lithuania, Malta, Poland, Slovak Republic and Slovenia. This should now make trading with these countries a little easier.

Some specific goods may require additional documentation and your chosen carrier may also have some paperwork to complete.

It is worth noting that when you send packages to dependencies of EU member states, such as the Falkland Islands, full customs documentation will be required.

Exporting worldwide

Opening up the world as your market place does entail more paperwork. When using the standard Royal Mail services, a simple customs label can be attached to the parcel; this contains a description of the item, the value, the weight and will be signed by yourself. If using another carrier for your items, there may be additional information required. The list below is just an example of some of the things that may be needed.

- **Import licence**
  As certain goods require an import licence, check with your importer that they have all the necessary documentation before you export your goods to them.

- **Export licence**
  Certain goods going to some countries will require an export licence from the Department of Trade and Industry. Contact the Export Control Organisation (www.dti.gov.uk/export.control/) for advice in this area.

- **Certificates of origin**
  Certificates of origin and movement certificates should be available from larger Chambers of Commerce. If the country you are trading with has a preferential trade agreement, you may receive reduced tariff rates or even duty free treatment.

- **VAT labels/Clearance**
  If you are exporting outside of the EU, each item over £100 must carry a VAT Label 444 on the outside of the package. These are available from your local Customs VAT Office.

- **Commercial invoice**
  If you are sending goods other than samples, gifts or possessions to destinations outside of the EU, three copies of a commercial invoice must accompany each package.

Who can help

For any advice relating to the shipment of goods overseas, contact the HM Customs and Excise National Advice Service (www.uktradeinfo.com) on 0845 0109 000.

Summary

You should now:

- understand eBay's **Shops** and **Seller tools**;

- understand why your **Feedback** is so important;

- know of several ways to **source stock cheaply**;

- understand what **affiliate sales** are;

- know how to become a **Power Seller**; and

- understand some of the paperwork required to **export** to the EU and worldwide.

If you are like me, you should find that the fun bit of eBay is the buying and the selling. But the supporting paperwork can't be ignored. So, if you can contain your excitement, legal issues and tax coming right up...

10

Managing the paperwork

Overview

Not surprisingly, you will find that there is a certain amount of administration required to run your own business. If nothing else, you will need to know how much profit you are making, so that you can alter your selling strategy accordingly. There is also the question of tax that may be due on any profits made through your eBay transactions.

As a seller on eBay, you have agreed to comply with all applicable domestic and international laws and regulations regarding your use of the eBay service; this is a condition of registration and applies to all of your listings.

You are also responsible for paying all fees associated with using the eBay site. This means that if you are trading as a business, then it is your responsibility to pay any taxes on your earnings. eBay will not manage this for you, and if asked by the HM Revenue & Customs, they will make information available to the tax office.

This section outlines the basics of managing your paperwork and covers the areas of taxation and self-employment. This is a complex area and tax situations are different for each individual, so it is important to seek professional guidance regarding your own circumstances.

Business plan

When you set out to trade on eBay, you may have a firm idea of where you want to go and have the necessary funding in place to achieve it. There may, however, come a time when you will need to convince other people that your business is a good prospect, for example, if you need to borrow money from a bank.

When this time comes, you will be expected to have a business plan of some description. Below I outline the basics of such a document.

What is a business plan?

Put simply, a business plan is a written document that sets out the future plans of a business and shows how it is planned to evolve and grow. A business plan will outline the goals for the future, what resources will be needed to achieve them and how the resources will be utilised. These resources could include people as well as accommodation and equipment. Above all, the business plan will tell the reader why the business will succeed.

What sort of things go into a business plan?

There is no fixed format for a business plan. The main thing is for it to contain the right elements presented in a concise way. Some of the elements that should be included are:

- **Executive summary**
  This will summarise the whole document into one or two pages and is intended for those readers who have little time to read through the whole document; if they like the executive summary, they will read any extra detail they need.

- **Introduction**
  An introduction or overview of the business or business idea. This should provide the reader with an insight as to where the business is now.

- **Competition**
  Provide the reader with an overview of the marketplace in which the business operates and any competition that it must face.

- **Services offered**
  In the case of an eBay business, this section is likely to contain details of products that are currently, or could be, sold via eBay as a route to market.

- **Strategy section**
  Outline the way in which the business will market its products, how it will price them and distribute them to the end customer. Maybe you will choose to advertise your eBay business in the traditional press or on the radio.

- **Financial plan**
  This section will include balance sheets, cash flow statements and

predictions for income and expenditure.

To expand on that final element, the financial plan includes:

- **Balance sheet**
  A balance sheet makes the comparison between what your business owns, its assets, against what it owes, its debts.

- **Cash flow statement**
  A cash flow statement shows how you intend to cope during periods when you will be buying stock and may not be selling it at the same rate. Preparing for the Christmas rush would be an example: you will buy lots of stock in the months before, but not receive any income from sales until some time later. The cash flow statement will show how you will manage this situation.

- **Income statement**
  An income statement will compare your income (sales from eBay), against expenditure (both stock purchase and business costs). This will demonstrate if you are actually going to make any money from the undertaking.

Having a business plan in place is a good idea even if you are not looking for additional finance. It will force you to focus on the hard facts of your business and allow you to take steps to correct things if they start to go wrong. If you don't have a plan for your business, how will you know if you are successful?

Legal concerns

The legal issues surrounding trading in any form can be quite complex, this section is intended only as a guide. You should consult a qualified professional if you are in any doubt as to the legality of your venture.

Buyers at online auctions have less protection under consumer law than through traditional retail outlets – the phrase *caveat emptor* (or 'buyer beware') holds true. However, there are some areas, such as the deliberate failure to send an item that has been purchased at auction, which are criminal offences. The Office of Fair Trading has a guide to help with these issues; you can see the full details on their website (www.oft.gov.uk).

Governing law and legal compliance

The eBay User Agreement states the conditions under which you have agreed to trade and details their position in areas such as the law and taxation. The full agreement can be found in the eBay help pages, I have copied below some of the main points.

Extracts from the eBay User Agreement

- This User Agreement shall be governed by and construed in accordance with English law and subject to the exclusive jurisdiction of the English courts.

- Please note, that your country (and/or that of any user you deal with) may have laws which apply to your transactions with other users regardless of what you agree with us (now) or with that user (later).

- The laws of your country may be different from English law, including laws governing what can be legally offered, sold, exported, bought or imported.

- There may be additional legal requirements, relating to (for example) the requirement to hold a licence to buy or sell certain items, or to register a transfer in a central registry. You shall comply with all applicable domestic and international laws, statutes, ordinances and regulations regarding your use of our service and your bidding on, listing, purchase and solicitation of offers to purchase and sale of items.

- There is no practical way for us (eBay) to continually monitor the laws of every country, or each user transaction. Please do not assume that you are allowed to do what other users do, or that we are approving or validating any transaction, even if you have successfully made similar sales or purchases in the past.

These few lines are really saying that it is down to the individual to ensure that they comply with all rules and legal requirements when trading. eBay will make certain help sections available and offer general advice, but cannot advise on an individual situation.

Taxation

As more and more trade is passed through eBay, the potential loss to the HM Revenue & Customs through unpaid taxes is set to rise. It is therefore quite likely that more attention will be given to traders on eBay by HM Revenue & Customs.

As a general rule, there is no tax liability on any money raised by selling your own items. So, clearing the house or garage of your own possessions should not interest the tax man. They will, however, be interested if you buy with the intention to sell – any profits from this activity are likely to be subject to tax.

The tax rules that apply to an individual could be very complex, and this is not the place to delve too deeply into the finer points of tax law. The responsibility lies with the individual to declare their activities to the HM Revenue & Customs.

There are three taxes to consider:

1. Income tax

2. Capital gains tax

3. VAT

These are explained below.

1. Income tax

Income tax is a ... tax on income – no surprises there! In the case of an eBay business, this is the profit, after expenses, on any difference between the buying and selling price.

The structure of income tax in the UK operates via a system of bands and allowances. Each individual has a personal allowance which is deducted from their total income in order to arrive at their taxable income. The first part of their income is **tax free**. The rest of a person's income is then **taxable** and is subject to different tax rates depending upon the *tax band* that income falls within. A summary of the current tax bands is given in the table overleaf.

Table 20: Income tax allowances

Income tax allowances	2005-06 (£)	2006-07 (£)
Personal allowance	4,895	5,035
Personal allowance for people aged 65-74	7,090	7,280
Personal allowance for people aged 75 and over	7,220	7,420
Income limit for age-related allowances	19,500	20,100
Married couple's allowance for people born before 6 April 1935	5,905	6,065
Married couple's allowance – aged 75 or more	5,975	6,135
Minimum amount of married couple's allowance	2,280	2,350
Blind person's allowance	1,610	1,660

Source – HM Revenue & Customs: (www.hmrc.gov.uk/rates/it.htm)

It is important to note that these earnings figures include all income for the year. If you are also employed, then both the income from your job and from eBay will count towards your total earnings.

Table 21: Income tax bands

Taxable bands allowances	2005-06 (£)	2006-07 (£)
Starting rate 10%	0 – 2,090	0 – 2,150
Basic rate 22%	2,090 – 32,400	2,150 – 33,300
Higher rate 40%	Over 32,400	over 33,300

Source – Inland Revenue (www.hmrc.gov.uk/rates/it.htm)

The actual level at which tax becomes payable, and the rate of that tax payment, will depend upon your personal situation. If you are in any doubt, contact the HM Revenue & Customs (www.hmrc.gov.uk) directly and they will advise on any issue.

2. Capital gains tax (CGT)

CGT is a tax on the increase in the capital value of an item. You normally only have to pay CGT when you no longer own an asset, that is, when you have disposed of it. This is HM Revenue & Customs' definition and the ruling applies to most assets that are bought and then sold for a higher value: it is the difference between the purchase and sale price that may be liable to tax.

Each individual has a personal allowance, which varies from year to year. There is also an indexation allowance calculator which is used for assets that were purchased some years ago. As a general rule, only high value items will be considered for capital gains. The HM Revenue & Customs leaflet 'Capital Gains Tax' (www.hmrc.gov.uk/leaflets/cgt1.htm) outlines the circumstances in which it might be paid.

For the tax year 2005-2006, the capital gains tax allowance for an individual was £8,500. For 2006-2007, it's £0,800.

3. VAT

If your taxable turnover, not just your profit, hits the current VAT threshold, or you expect it to, you must register with HM Customs and Excise for VAT. VAT is a tax on consumer expenditure and is collected on business transactions.

Most business transactions involve the supply of goods or services. VAT is payable if they are:

- supplies made in the United Kingdom or the Isle of Man;

- by a taxable person;

- in the course of a business; and

- are not specifically exempted or zero-rated.

If your business exceeds the taxable turnover level, or you expect it to, contact the Customs and Excise helpline on 0845 010 9000.

eBay offer some advice on this area, however, the burden of responsibility rests with the individual. I have extracted some of the key points regarding VAT.

Extracts from eBay advice on VAT

- Laws and regulations dealing with VAT on sales transactions are complicated. These laws and regulations address, for example, whether a seller's business should be registered for VAT, whether a seller is required to charge VAT on sold items, and, if so, how much VAT should be charged on those items.

- For the above reason, a seller should consult an independent tax advisor and/or local tax authority to determine what laws and rules apply, including whether a business should be registered and whether and how much VAT is required to be charged on an item.

- For UK sellers, as a first research step, a seller may find it useful to consult the HM Customs and Excise Web Site, which addresses certain aspects of VAT and VAT registration.

- As an online marketplace, eBay leaves the decision to the seller as to whether and how VAT should be charged on an item. eBay however does require the seller to adhere to all applicable VAT laws and regulations in listing an item on www.eBay.co.uk.

- In the item description, the seller should set out clearly the amount or percentage of VAT that will be charged.

- If there is no mention of VAT in the item description, the seller should not add VAT to the final item price. In such a case, if VAT is legally due, the seller bears the responsibility of paying that VAT to the appropriate authorities according to any applicable laws and regulations. Again, if there is any question as to the seller's VAT responsibilities, the seller should consult an independent tax advisor and/or local tax authority.

Self-employment

Once your activities on eBay have reached a certain level, it may be the time to register as self-employed. This will probably occur when you have sold all of your own personal items and decide to begin trading: buying with the intention to sell for a profit.

This can seem daunting and there may be a temptation to continue as before. However the process is not too difficult and there are some benefits as well. In this section I will expand on the topic of becoming self-employed. As mentioned before, I cannot be specific about personal tax situations as they will vary from person to person. If you need to confirm your own circumstances, check the HM Revenue & Customs website:

www.hmrc.gov.uk/startingup/

What does it mean?

Becoming self-employed on eBay simply means that you intend to buy and sell for profit. As with any earned income, you will need to declare this to the HM Revenue & Customs. It also means that any costs involved with your eBay activities can be offset against your profit, as it is the figure after the deduction of costs that may be liable to income tax.

Self employment is just the way to capture all the details of your eBay activities and record them in a simple way.

You can be self-employed and also work full or part-time. All of your net income is added together and income tax is applied depending upon your personal circumstances. If eBay is to be your only source of income, then you can earn up to your personal tax free allowance, which is approximately £5,000, before paying any tax.

How do I register?

The first thing to do is register with the HM Revenue & Customs. There is naturally a booklet about it – 'Thinking of Working for Yourself'. This contains some basic information and a registration form; just fill it in and return it. The form should be completed within three months of the date you began working for yourself. Alternatively you can access the form online at:

www.hmrc/startingup/register.htm

HM Revenue & Customs will then send a 'Starter Pack' with more details. This form will also cover the issues surrounding National Insurance contributions.

National Insurance

National Insurance contributions build up your entitlements to various benefits, such as unemployment benefit and the state retirement pension.

There are several different types of National Insurance contributions that you might have to pay. For the self-employed, there are four main types – summarised in the table below with figures for the 2006/7 tax year.

It is also worth noting that if your expected earnings for the year fall below a certain amount, you may be eligible for an exemption from Class 2 payments. To apply for this exemption, just contact the HM Revenue & Customs and – you've guessed it - there is a form to fill in.

Table 22: National Insurance contributions

National Insurance contribution class	Who has to pay it?	You pay it if...	On what income?	How is it collected?
Class 1	People who are employed (note: you can be employed and self-employed at the same time).	You have earned more than £97/week.	On your earnings as an employee.	Out of your pay, through your employers.
Class 2	People who are self-employed.	There is no relationship with your income, you pay a flat rate contribution.		By the National Insurance Contributions Office, usually through direct debit.
Class 3	Nobody has to – this is a voluntary contribution.	You choose to do so, to qualify for pension benefits that you would otherwise lose. There is no relationship with your income – you pay a flat rate contribution every week.		By the National Insurance Contributions Office, usually through direct debit.
Class 4	Self-employed people who make more than a certain amount of profits.	You have made profits of more than £5,035 during the year.	On your profits.	Through the tax payments you make after filling in your self-assessment tax form.

Source: HM Revenue & Customs

How to record your business activities

When you have been trading for some time, you will need to submit details of your eBay trading to the HM Revenue & Customs. This is most likely to occur at the end of the tax year in April. If you have kept some simple records during the year, you will only have to copy a few figures to your tax return. HM Revenue & Customs are unlikely to want to see your detailed records.

How you record your business activities is really down to personal choice. There are some computer packages available or you could consult an accountant. You could also create your own spreadsheet or just write them down on paper. You must decide how best to do this, but once you have settled on a method, keep them up to date and filling in the tax return will be much easier.

If you don't have any business management software, you can of course use eBay to help you keep track of your sales. In your 'My eBay', you probably already use the sold section to see how your items are selling; these details can be printed out to provide a permanent record of trading activity. You can customise the content of the report and use this to compile your trading figures for the year.

At this time I do not use any management software to compile my accounts; my turnover is such that a simple spreadsheet is sufficient. I do however use my primary trading ID to sell personal items that I no longer need. These items do not form part of my eBay business and need to be removed from the sales total.

I have found that printing the sales on a monthly basis works well for me. I can then update my spreadsheet during a quiet time, including my trading costs and expenses. This will in turn provide my trading figures for my tax return.

This system is a little labour intensive, but it works for me at the moment. If I decide to increase turnover in the coming months, I will invest in a management program. As with all things connected with an eBay business, it is a case of evolution, which includes the accounting aspects.

How to work out your business profit

There are three main elements that will determine how your business performs. These form your trading account and will determine if you have made a profit or a loss.

1. You will make sales via eBay, and the value of these when added together will produce your *turnover*.

2. The items you sell will cost you something to purchase, the total value of these will be your cost of sales. When you deduct the *cost of your sales* from the turnover you will have calculated your *gross profit*.

3. Just buying and selling is only part of the picture. It will cost you something to sell your goods and it will have cost you something to buy them in the first place (e.g. the cost of the internet connection, eBay fees), these are your expenses. When the expenses are deducted from the gross profit, you will end up with a net profit figure. This is the true profit that you have made and it is this figure upon which you may have to pay tax and National Insurance.

Typical expenses of an eBay business

The true cost of selling in any business will vary. There are the costs of the stock and the cost of actually selling and running the business. With an eBay business, the costs can be quite varied, although there are some that would apply to almost all businesses.

These expenses of your business will reduce the amount of profit you make from your trading activities, so it is important to record them all. It is also important not to inflate them as this may cause problems when you submit your tax return.

Typical expenses will include:

- Packing materials

- Stamps

- Staff wages

- Heat and light

- Insurance

- Fuel costs

- Stationary costs (paper, ink)

- Telephone lines

- Bank charges

- eBay charges

- PayPal charges

- Rent

- Training

In addition to these running costs, your business will also need some equipment before it can trade. The list of items will vary, but is likely to include:

- Computers

- Printers

- Mobile phone

You may also have buildings that are used for your business, maybe for storage, these need to be purchased and maintained as well.

Summary

You should now:

- understand the broad **terms of trading** under eBay's User Agreement;

- have a broad understanding of the implications of **income tax, CGT and VAT** on your trading business;

- know how to register as **self-employed**; and

- know what are the typical **expenses** of an eBay business.

Conclusion

Welcome to the conclusion of the book, and well done for making it this far!

I hope that these pages have been of interest and will increase your eBay profits significantly. A career in any business takes time to develop, and eBay is no different. Throughout my eBay journey, there have been several high points and many lessons to learn, most of which are contained in this book, so that you don't fall foul of them.

I also intend to develop further my own eBay business over the coming months. This includes opening an eBay Shop, redesigning my workshop preparation and storage processes and completely re-inventing my photography skills, so this is only really the end of the beginning.

The great thing about an eBay business is that you can take it at your own pace. If you found a place in the book that suits you, stop there for a while and see how things go. You should now be able to approach selling on eBay with a new focus.

The chapter on the listing process is quite detailed and some practice will be needed to present items correctly. But stick with it, the difference it will make to your sales cannot be overstated. The chapters concerning the supply of stock, pre and post sales processes, coupled with the numerous sales tips along the way, should ensure that you have an edge on your competition.

Please try some of the HTML codes – it is a little like learning a new language. Loading the large pictures and creating your own template border should save you more than the cost of this book in a matter of days.

Where should you go for more help?

There are always things to learn and there will always be somebody willing to assist. If you do need more advice, access the community discussion boards or use the navigation techniques you will have picked up from this book to find your way through the maze of eBay help pages.

Why not subscribe to my free weekly newsletter at www.ebaybulletin.co.uk which contains the latest gossip from eBay and loads of hints and tips from the trading experience of myself and others. (There are more details on the newsletter at the back of this book.)

eBay is bound to grow, at least for the foreseeable future; the television advertising will help with this, but it is word of mouth that will drive the increase in its popularity. What a fantastic time to begin your own business, with almost no capital outlay required, a work pattern that suits your own lifestyle and rewards that are limited only by your own actions. To work for yourself and be at the forefront of the eBay revolution, I say revolution and I mean it, eBay will completely change the way commerce is conducted in the UK and the expectations that people have from their working lives.

Welcome to The Good Life

I have fully embraced the lifestyle: the late nights before Christmas packing parcels and the extra coffee breaks during the day. I have travelled from a standing start to leaving full-time work within two years – and anybody can do this. As I have said, selling on eBay is not difficult. It is the contents of this book that will place you ahead of the crowd as we rush headlong into a brave new world where every household has an eBay account and the first place you look to buy anything is eBay.

I would like to wish you every success in your future trading and that it brings to you, as it has to me, a glimpse of "The Good Life".

Appendices

Prohibited items

The items below are prohibited for sale on eBay.

Aeroplane Tickets	Lock-picking Devices
Alcohol	Lottery Tickets
Animals and wildlife products	Mailing Lists and Personal
Catalogue and URL Sales	Information
Counterfeit Currency and Stamps	Multi-level Marketing, Pyramid,
Counterfeit and Trademarked Items	Matrix and Trading Schemes
Credit Cards	Offensive Material
Drugs and Drug paraphernalia	Prescription Drugs and Materials
Embargoed Items & Prohibited	Recalled Items
Countries	Satellite, Digital and Cable TV
Firearms and Ammunition	Decoders
Fireworks	Shares and Securities
Franking Machines	Stolen Items
Football Tickets	Surveillance Equipment
Government IDs, Licences and	Tobacco and Tobacco Products
Uniforms	Train Tickets
Human Parts and Remains	Travel Vouchers
	Unlocking Software

Questionable items

Adults Only	Hazardous, Restricted and
Artefacts	Perishable Items
Autographed Items	Pesticides
Batteries	Plants and Seeds
British Titles	Police-Related Items
CFC and HCFC Refrigerants	Pre sales Listings
Contracts and Tickets	Slot Machines
Electronics Equipment	Used Clothing
Food	Used Medical Devices
	Weapons & Knives

Potentially infringing items

Academic Software	Image or Description Theft
Anti-circumvention Policy	Importation of Goods
Authenticity Disclaimers	Keyword Spamming
Beta Software	Misleading Titles
Bootleg Recordings	Mod Chips
Brand Name Misuse	Movie Prints
Comparison Policy	OEM Software
Compilation and Informational	Recordable Media
Media Policy	Replica and Counterfeit Items
Copyright Basics	Promotional Items
Downloadable Media	Trademark and Domain Name
Encouraging Infringement Policy	Basics
Faces, Names and Signatures	Unauthorized Copies
Games Software	

Sample terms & conditions statement

Below are some suggestions for a typical set of trading terms and conditions (T&C). Use them as a basis to compile your own set and amend any areas that don't quite fit the way you will operate your business.

The T&C can be placed within each listing or on a separate page if you are using links in your listings. The 'About Me' page is a great place to put them as well. You can also include clickable links in the T&C to the Royal Mail and other courier websites, enabling bidders to check postal and insurance costs.

Trading terms and conditions – The small print

Payment timescales

I do not have a fixed time period for payment, but the sooner I receive payment, the sooner I will dispatch your item. I will send a courtesy email after a week or so to check that all is well, sometimes payments do go missing. If I have not heard anything after 4 weeks, I will have to start the process to recover my fees from eBay, but will keep you informed at each stage.

Payment and postage

Within the UK

- **Payment**
  I would be happy to accept payment via the following methods: Personal cheque, PayPal, postal orders and bank transfer.

- **Postage timescale**
  Please allow up to 5 working days for cheques to clear. I will send items within 2 working days if payment is received by other methods.

I will send parcels up to 1 kilo in weight via Royal Mail standard post, items over 1 kilo will be sent by standard parcel post.

I obtain a **proof of posting** for all parcels sent.

If you would like to **insure your parcel**, please just let me know or check out the Royal Mail website for costs.

I will **confirm** via email when your item has been dispatched.

Outside of the UK

* **Payment**
  I would be happy to accept payment via the following methods: PayPal, personal check in American Dollars, Euros or Australian Dollars, international bank transfer and money orders that are negotiable within the UK.

* **Postage timescale**
  Please allow up to two weeks for cheque clearance. I will send items paid for by other methods within 2 days of receipt of payment.

My standard shipping option is via Royal Mail airmail. Surface mail is also available, please email me for more details.

If you would like to **insure your parcel,** please let me know or check out the Royal Mail website for options and costs.

I will confirm via email when your item has been dispatched.

General postage information

My postage costs are based on the weight and dimensions of the item, including packaging, as per the UK Royal Mail published costs. They also include all packing materials used to ship your item.

Returns

If for any reason the item is not as described in the auction listing, I would be happy to offer a full refund upon return of the item in the original packing. The return postage costs would not be included in any refund made. If you feel that the item is not as it should be for any other reason, please just let me know and I will sort something out.

Spoof emails

Email 1: PayPal account hijack

Security Center Advisory!

We recently noticed one or more attempts to log in to your PayPal account from a foreign IP address and we have reasons to belive that your account was hijacked by a third party without your authorization. If you recently accessed your account while traveling, the unusual log in attempts may have been initiated by you.

If you are the rightful holder of the account you must **click the link below** and then complete all steps from the following page as we try to verify your identity.

Click here to verify your account

If you choose to ignore our request, you leave us no choise but to temporaly suspend your account.

Thank you for using PayPal! The PayPal Team
Please do not reply to this e-mail. Mail sent to this address cannot be answered. For assistance, log in to your PayPal account and choose the 'Help' link in the footer of any page.

To receive email notifications in plain text instead of HTML, update your preferences here.

PayPal Email ID PP697

Protect Your Account Info

Make sure you never provide your password to fraudulent persons.

PayPal automatically encrypts your confidential information using the Secure Sockets Layer protocol (SSL) with an encryption key length of 128-bits (the highest level commercially available).

PayPal will never ask you to enter your password in an email.

For more information on protecting yourself from fraud, please review our Security Tips at http://www.paypal.com/us/
Protect Your Password
You should never give your PayPal password to anyone, including PayPal employees.

Email 2: eBay account hijack

Update Your Account Information Within 24 Hours

Valued eBay Member,

According to our site policy you will have to confirm that you are the real owner of the eBay account by completing the following form or else your account will be suspended within 24 hours for investigations.

Never share your eBay password to anyone!

Establish your proof of identity with ID Verify (free of charge) - an easy way to help others trust you as their trading partner. The process takes about 5 minutes to complete and involves updating your eBay information. When you're successfully verified, you will receive an ID Verify icon 🆔 in your feedback profile. Currently, the service is only available to residents of the United States and U.S. territories (Puerto Rico, US Virgin Islands and Guam.)

To update your eBay records >> *Click here* <<

We appreciate your support and understanding, as we work together to keep eBay a safe place to trade. Thank you for your patience in this matter.

Trust and Safety Department
eBay Inc.

Please do not reply to this e-mail as this is only a notification. Mail sent to this address cannot be answered.

Note : Ignoring this message will cause the Suspension of your account . To reactivate it you will have to pay a fee of 350 $.

Copyright 1995-2004 eBay Inc. All Rights Reserved. Designated trademarks and brands are the property of their respective owners. Use of this Web site constitutes acceptance of the eBay User Agreement and Privacy Policy. Designated trademarks and brands are the property of their respective owners. eBay and the eBay logo are trademarks of eBay Inc. eBay is located at 2145 Hamilton Avenue, San Jose, CA 95125.

Email 3: eBay account hijack

Congratulations! You've earned the honor of joining the eBay Silver PowerSeller Program. Come and join us. When you join the PowerSeller program, you'll be able to receive more of the support you'll need for continued success. So, why wait? Join now !

What are the benefits?

PowerSeller icon next to your User ID in recognition of your hard work.

PowerSeller Priority Support via email webform and phone support at Silver level and above.

Exclusive offerings on the PowerSeller portal--check in frequently to see updated program benefits and special offers!

Discussion Board for you to network with other PowerSellers.

Free PowerSeller Business Templates for business cards and letterhead.

Regards,
eBay PowerSeller Team
If you agree with this rank please Become an eBay Power Seller within 24 hours

eBay sent this communication to you because of your outstanding feedback, high sales, and compliance with eBay marketplace policies. If you would not like to be invited to join the PowerSeller program, follow the directions above, click "Member Sign In", and then click "Decline" at the bottom of the page. Please note that it may take up to 10 days to process your request.

Copyright © 2005 eBay Inc. All Rights Reserved.
Designated trademarks and brands are the property of their respective owners.
eBay and the eBay logo are trademarks of eBay Inc.
eBay is located at 2145 Hamilton Avenue, San Jose, CA 95125.

➥ *Go to the PowerSellers Portal*

invitationReminder_header_j-1.gif

invitationReminder_headerBT-1.gif

What are the benefits?

ubheader_whatAreTheBenefits-1.gif

Quick reference postal rates

Inland postal costs – First Class

Format	Size	Weight	After 21st August 2006	Before 21st August 2006
Letters	Max 240x165mm 5mm thick	0 - 100g	32p	32 - 49p
Large Letters	Max 353x250mm 25mm thick	0 - 100g	44p	32p - £2.89
		101 - 250g	65p	
		251 - 500g	90p	
		501 - 750g	131p	
Packets	Any item over 353mm long OR 250mm wide OR over 25mm thick	0 - 100g	100p	32p - £4.74
		101g - 250g	127p	
		251g - 500g	170p	
		501g - 750g	220p	
		751g - 1kg	270p	
		1001 - 1250g	474p	
		1250g+	+85p for each additional 250g or part thereof	

Inland postal costs – Second Class

Format	Size	Weight	After 21st August 2006	Before 21st August 2006
Letters	Max 240x165mm 5mm thick	0 - 100g	23p	23 - 37p
Large Letters	Max 353x250mm 25mm thick	0 - 100g	37p	23p - £2.12
		101 - 250g	55p	
		251 - 500g	75p	
		501 - 750g	109p	
Packets	Any item over 353mm long OR 250mm wide OR over 25mm thick	0 - 100g	84p	23p - £2.12
		101g - 250g	109p	
		251g - 500g	139p	
		501g - 750g	177p	
		751g - 1kg	212p	
		1001 - 1250g	n/a	
		1250g+	n/a	

Inland Parcels standard rates August 21st 2006

Maximum weight	Price
1kg	£3.85
1.5kg	£4.95
2kg	£5.31
4kg	£7.70
6kg	£8.74
8kg	£9.97
10kg	£10.70
20kg	£12.46

International airmail rates

Weight not over	Letters			Small packets		Printed papers	
	Europe	World Zone 1	World Zone 2	Europe	World Zone 1 and 2	Europe	World Zone 1 and 2
Postcards		£0.50	£0.50				
10g	£0.44	£0.50	£0.50				
20g	£0.44	£0.72	£0.72				
40g	£0.64	£1.12	£1.19				
60g	f0.83	£1.51	£1.66				
80g	£1.02	£1.91	£2.14				
100g	£1.21	£2.31	£2.61	f1.10	£1.46	£0.95	£1.44
120g	£1.41	£2.70	£3.08	£1.21	£1.66	£1.04	£1.65
140g	£1.60	£3.10	£3.55	£1.33	£1.87	£1.14	1.87
160g	£1.79	£3.49	£4.02	£1.45	£2.07	£1.24	£2.08
180g	£1.99	£3.89	£4.49	£1.57	£2.27	£1.33	£2.30
200g	£2.17	£4.29	£4.96	£1.69	£2.48	£1.43	£2.51
220g	£2.35	£4.66	£5.40	£1.80	£2.67	£1.53	£2.71
240g	£2.53	£5.03	£5.84	£1.91	£2.86	£1.62	£2.91
260g	£2.71	£5.40	£6.28	£2.02	£3.05	£1.72	£3.11
280g	£2.89	£5.77	£6.72	£2.12	£3.24	£1.81	£3.31
300g	£3.08	£6.14	£7.16	£2.23	£3.43	£1.92	£3.51

Weight not over	Letters			Small packets		Printed papers	
	Europe	World Zone 1	World Zone 2	Europe	World Zone 1 and 2	Europe	World Zone 1 and 2
320g	£3.25	£6.51	£7.60	£2.29	£3.62	£2.03	£3.71
340g	£3.43	£6.88	£8.04	£2.39	£3.81	£2.13	£3.91
360g	£3.61	£7.25	£8.48	£2.49	£4.00	£2.23	£4.11
380g	£3.79	£7.62	£8.92	£2.59	£4.19	£2.33	£4.31
400g	£3.97	£7.99	£9.36	£2.69	£4.38	£2.43	£4.51
420g	£4.15	£8.36	£9.80	£2.79	£4.57	£2.53	£4.71
440g	£4.33	£8.73	£10.24	£2.89	£4.76	£2.63	£4.91
460g	£4.51	£9.10	£10.68	£2.99	£4.95	£2.73	£5.11
480g	£4.69	£9.47	£11.12	£3.09	£5.14	£2.83	£5.31
500g	£4.87	£9.84	£11.56	£3.19	£5.33	£2.93	£5.51
520g	£5.05	£10.21	£12.00	£3.29	£5.52	£3.03	£5.71
540g	£5.23	£10.58	£12.44	£3.39	£5.71	£3.13	£5.91
560g	£5.41	£10.95	£12.88	£3.49	£5.90	£3.23	£6.11
580g	£5.59	£11.32	£13.32	£3.59	£6.09	£3.33	£6.31
600g	£5.77	£11.69	£13.76	£3.69	£6.28	£3.43	£6.51
620g	£5.95	£12.06	£14.20	£3.79	£6.47	£3.53	£6.71
640g	£6.13	£12.43	£14.64	£3.89	£6.66	£3.63	£6.91

Weight not over	Letters			Small packets		Printed paper	
	Europe	World Zone 1	World Zone 2	Europe	World Zone 1 and 2	Europe	World Zone 1 and 2
660g	£6.31	£12.80	£15.08	£3.99	£6.85	£3.73	£7.11
680g	£6.49	£13.17	£15.52	£4.09	£7.04	£3.83	£7.31
700g	£6.67	£13.54	£15.96	£4.19	£7.23	£3.93	£7.51
720g	£6.85	£13.91	£16.40	£4.29	£7.42	£4.03	£7.71
740g	£7.03	£14.28	£16.84	£4.39	£7.61	£4.13	£7.91
760g	£7.21	£14.65	£17.28	£4.49	£7.80	£4.23	£8.11
780g	£7.39	£15.02	£17.72	£4.59	£7.99	£4.33	£8.31
800g	£7.57	£15.39	£18.16	£4.69	£8.18	£4.43	£8.51
820g	£7.75	£15.76	£18.60	£4.79	£8.37	£4.53	£8.71
840g	£7.93	£16.13	£19.04	£4.89	£8.56	£4.63	£8.91
860g	£8.11	£16.50	£19.48	£4.99	£8.75	£4.73	£9.11
880g	£8.29	£16.87	£19.92	£5.09	£8.94	£4.83	£9.31
900g	£8.47	£17.24	£20.36	£5.19	£9.13	£4.93	£9.51
920g	£8.65	£17.61	£20.80	£5.29	£9.32	£5.03	£9.71
940g	£8.83	£17.98	£21.24	£5.39	£9.51	£5.13	£9.91
960g	£9.01	£18.35	£21.68	£5.49	£9.70	£5.23	£10.11

Weight not over	Letters			Small packets		Printed paper	
	Europe	World Zone 1	World Zone 2	Europe	World Zone 1 and 2	Europe	World Zone1 and 2
980g	£9.19	£18.72	£22.12	£5.59	£9.89	£5.33	£10.31
1000g	£9.37	£19.09	£22.56	£5.69	£10.08	£5.43	£10.51
1020g	£9.55	£19.46	£23.00	£5.79	£10.27	£5.52	£10.71
1040g	£9.73	£19.83	£23.44	£5.89	£10.46	£5.61	£10.91
1060g	£9.91	£20.20	£23.88	£5.99	£10.65	£5.70	£11.11
1080g	£10.09	£20.57	£24.32	£6.09	£10.84	£5.79	£11.31
1100g	£10.27	£20.94	£24.76	£6.19	£11.03	£5.88	£11.51
1120g	£10.45	£21.31	£25.20	£6.29	£11.22	£5.97	£11.71
1140g	£10.63	£21.68	£25.64	£6.39	£11.41	£6.06	£11.91
1160g	£10.81	£22.05	£26.08	£6.49	£11.60	£6.15	£12.11
1180g	£10.99	£22.42	£26.52	£6.59	£11.79	£6.24	£12.31
1200g	£11.17	£22.79	£26.96	£6.69	£11.98	£6.33	£12.51
1220g	£11.35	£23.16	£27.40	£6.79	£12.17	£6.42	£12.71
1240g	£11.53	£23.53	£28.28	£6.89	£12.36	£6.51	£12.91
1260g	£11.71	£23.90	£28.72	£6.99	£12.55	£6.60	£13.11
1280g	£11.89	£24.27	£29.16	£7.09	£12.74	£6.69	£13.31

Weight not over	Letters			Small packets		Printed paper	
	Europe	World Zone 1	World Zone 2	Europe	World Zone 1 and 2	Europe	World Zone 1 and 2
1300g	£12.07	£24.64	£29.16	£7.19	£12.93	£6.78	£13.51
1320g	£12.25	£25.01	£29.60	£7.29	£13.12	£6.87	£13.71
1340g	£12.43	£25.38	£30.04	£7.39	£13.31	£6.96	£13.91
1360g	£12.61	£25.75	£30.48	£7.49	£13.50	£7.05	£14.11
1380g	£12.79	£26.12	£30.92	£7.59	£13.69	£7.14	£14.31
1400g	£12.97	£26.49	£31.36	£7.69	£13.88	£7.23	£14.51
1420g	£13.15	£26.86	£31.80	£7.79	£14.07	£7.32	£14.71
1440g	£13.33	£27.23	£32.24	£7.89	£14.26	£7.41	£14.91
1460g	£13.51	£27.60	£32.68	£7.99	£14.45	£7.50	£15.11
1480g	£13.69	£27.97	£33.12	£8.09	£14.64	£7.59	£15.31
1500g	£13.87	£28.34	£33.56	£8.19	£14.83	£7.68	£15.51
1520g	£14.05	£28.71	£34.00	£8.29	£15.02	£7.77	£15.71
1540g	£14.23	£29.08	£34.44	£8.39	£15.21	£7.86	£15.91

Weight not over	Letters			Small packets		Printed paper	
	Europe	World Zone 1	World Zone 2	Europe	World Zone 1 and 2	Europe	World Zone 1 and 2
1560g	£14.41	£29.45	£34.88	£8.49	£15.40	£7.95	£16.11
1580g	£14.59	£29.82	£35.32	£8.59	£15.59	£8.04	£16.31
1600g	£14.77	£30.19	£35.76	£8.69	£15.78	£8.13	£16.51
1620g	£14.95	£30.56	£36.20	£8.79	£15.97	£8.22	£16.71
1640g	£15.13	£30.93	£36.64	£8.89	£16.16	£8.31	£16.91
1660g	£15.31	£31.30	£37.08	£8.99	£16.35	£8.40	£17.11
1680g	£15.49	£31.67	£37.52	£9.09	£16.54	£8.49	£17.31
1700g	£15.67	£32.04	£37.96	£9.19	£16.73	£8.58	£17.51
1720g	£15.85	£32.41	£38.40	£9.29	£16.92	£8.67	£17.71
1740g	£16.03	£32.78	£38.84	£9.39	£17.11	£8.76	£17.91
1760g	£16.21	£33.15	£39.28	£9.49	£17.30	£8.85	£18.11
1780g	£16.39	£33.52	£39.72	£9.59	£17.49	£8.94	£18.31
1800g	£16.57	£33.89	£40.16	£9.69	£17.68	£9.03	£18.51
1820g	£16.75	£34.26	£40.60	£9.79	£17.87	£9.12	£18.71

Weight not over	Letters			Small packets		Printed paper	
	Europe	World Zone 1	World Zone 2	Europe	World Zone 1 and 2	Europe	World Zone 1 and 2
1840g	£16.93	£34.63	£41.04	£9.89	£18.06	9.21	£18.91
1860g	£17.11	£35.00	£41.48	£9.99	£18.25	£9.30	£19.11
1880g	£17.29	£35.37	£41.92	£10.09	£18.44	£9.39	£19.31
1900g	£17.47	£35.74	£42.36	£10.19	£18.63	£9.48	£19.51
1920g	£17.65	£36.11	£42.80	£10.29	£18.82	£9.57	£19.71
1940g	£17.83	£36.48	£43.24	£10.39	£19.01	£9.66	£19.91
1960g	£18.01	£36.85	£43.68	£10.49	£19.20	£9.75	£20.11
1980g	£18.19	£37.22	£44.12	£10.59	£19.39	£9.84	£20.31
2000g	£18.37	£37.59	£44.56	£10.69	£19.59	£9.93	£20.51

International surface mail rates

Weight not over	Letters	Small packets and printed papers
	World Zone 1 and 2	All destinations
Postcards	42p	
20g	42p	71p
60g	72p	71p
100g	£1.02	71p
150g	£1.43	96p
200g	£1.84	£1.20
250g	£2.24	£1.44
300g	£2.64	£1.68
350g	£3.04	£1.92
400g	£3.44	£2.16
450g	£3.84	£2.40
500g	£4.24	£2.64
550g	£4.64	£2.88
600g	£5.04	£3.12
650g	£5.44	£3.36
700g	£5.84	£3.60
750g	£6.24	£3.84
800g	£6.64	£4.08
850g	£7.04	£4.32
900g	£7.44	£4.56
950g	£7.84	£4.80
1000g	£8.24	£5.04
1050g	£8.64	£5.28
1100g	£9.04	£5.52
1150g	£9.44	£5.76
1200g	£9.84	£6.00
1250g	£10.24	£6.24
1300g	£10.64	£6.48
1350g	£11.04	£6.72
1400g	£11.44	£6.96
1450g	£11.84	£7.20
1500g	£12.24	£7.44
1550g	£12.64	£7.68
1600g	£13.04	£7.92
1650g	£13.44	£8.16
1700g	£13.84	£8.40
1750g	£14.24	£8.64
1800g	£14.64	£8.88
1850g	£15.04	£9.12
1900g	£15.44	£9.36
1950g	£15.84	£9.60
2000g	£16.24	£9.84

All the essential internet links in one place

Throughout the book I have made reference to internet web addresses that are essential for your eBay business. In this Appendix I have listed them all for quick reference.

Computer suppliers

Hewlett Packard (www.hp.com)

Packard Bell (www.packardbell.co.uk)

Dell (www.dell.co.uk)

Digital cameras

Comet (www.comet.co.uk)

Pixmania (www.pixmania.co.uk)

ebuyer (www.ebuyer.com)

Camera Memory cards: (www.picstop.co.uk)

Explanation of camera memory
(www.pcphotoreview.com/memoryguidecrx.aspx)

Internet access

Online Broadband checker (www.broadbandchecker.co.uk)

Broadband suppliers

BT Broadband (www.bt.com/broadband)

Tiscali (www.tiscali.co.uk)

AOL (www.aol.co.uk)

Virgin (www.virgin.net)

Wanadoo (www.wanadoo.co.uk)

Onetel (www.onetel.co.uk)

NTL (www.home.ntl.com)

Telewest (www.telewest.co.uk)

Satellite Broadband via AVC (www.avcbroadband.com)

Software

Anti virus software: PestPatrol (www.pestpatrol.com)

Auction design templates

Alou Web Design (www.alouwebdesign.ca/free-ebay-templates.htm)

Auction Insights (auctioninsights.com/practice/auction-template.html)

Auction Supplies (auctionsupplies.com/templates/)

Web Craft Creations
(www.webcraftscreations.com/web-design/ebay-web-site-design.html)

Online currency converters

Bloomberg (www.bloomberg.com/analysis/calculators/currency.html)

Yahoo Finance (finance.yahoo.com/currency)

Oanda.com (www.oanda.com/convert/classic)

eBay (pages.ebay.co.uk/services/buyandsell/currencyconverter.html)

Language translators

Altavista Babelfish (babelfish.altavista.com/babelfish/tr)

Free Translation (www.freetranslation.com)

Internet web hosting services

50 Megs (www.50megs.com)

Bravenet (www.bravenet.com)

Postal services

Royal Mail (www.royalmail.com)

Online payments companies

PayPal: (www.paypal.com)

Nochex: (www.nochex.com)

WorldPay: (www.worldpay.com)

Payments

Payments comparison site from The Deptartment of Trade & Industry (www.electronic-payments.co.uk)

Escrow: (www.escrow.com)

Photo-editing software

Serif PhotoPlus 6 (www.freeserifsoftware.com)

GIMP (www.gimp.org)

Ultimate Paint (www.ultimatepaint.com)

Pixia (park18.wakwak.com/~pixia/)

ImageForge (www.cursorarts.com)

Digital photography guides

www.vividlight.com/articles/3016.htm

www.betterphoto.com/article.asp?id=39

www.pcworld.com/howto/article/0,aid,112658,00.asp

www.imaging-resource.com

Cut, copy and paste references

www.webmasternow.com/copyandpaste.html

www.worldstart.com/tips/shared/copypaste.htm

Free online picture hosting companies

www.Photobucket.com

www.Tinypic.com

Fraud

UK Police Service (www.police.uk)

Other online auction sites:

Yahoo Auctions (auctions.yahoo.com)

Amazon Auctions (s1.amazon.com)

UBid (www.ubid.com)

Bidz.com (ht.bidz.com)

Affiliate sales

Commission Junction (www.cj.com)

Tax and law

Department of Trade and Industry - Export Control (www.dti.gov.uk/export.control/)

HM Revenue & Customs General (www.hmrc.gov.uk)

Capital Gains Tax (www.hmrc.gov.uk/leaflets/cgt1.htm)

Self-employment (www.hmrc.gov.uk/startingup/index.htm)

Glossary of terms and abbreviations

Throughout eBay many abbreviations are used to save time and space, particularly in the restricted title box. This list is by no means complete but, it contains those terms that are more common and the ones we feel are in common use and more pertinent to selling.

BIN
Buy It Now

BNWT
Brand New With Tag

Browse
How to find general items.

Dutch Auction
Used when offering multiple items that are identical for sale. Multiple item auctions can have many winners, all of which pay the same price, which is the lowest successful bid.

FVF
Final Value Fee

Gallery
The small picture which can sit alongside the item title in the search results page.

HTML
Hypertext Markup Language

ISP
Internet Service Provider

Inventory
The stock you have for sale or awaiting sale.

JPG
Pronounced J-Peg, this is a file format for pictures.

Keyword spamming
Using top search words within your auction to attract visitors that do not relate to any aspect of your auction.

Link
Text or a picture that sits on a web page, usually the description or 'About Me' page, that if clicked will take you to another page of the internet. Also known as 'hyperlink'.

MIB
Mint In Box

Mint
The item is in perfect condition.

MIP
Mint in Packet

MOC
Mint on Card

NARU
Not A Registered User, a suspended account.

NR
No Reserve

NPB
Non-Paying Bidder

Newbie
Somebody who is new to eBay.

OOP
Out of Print or Production

PayPal
An eBay company, allowing buyers and sellers to send and receive money via an electronic medium.

Reserve
The price below which the item will not sell even if it has bids.

ROI
Return on Investment

SYI

Sell Your Item. Usually refers to the form.

Search

How to find specific items.

Second Chance

A feature of all standard auction listings that will allow you to make offers to any under-bidders at their highest bid price.

Sig

Signature

Spam

Unwanted emails often offering items for sale without the receivers consent.

URL

Uniform Resource Locator. The address for the web page

VHTF

Very Hard To Find

Vintage

Goods produced before 1980.

Index

A

B

Sign up to the FREE eBay UK Bulletin

If this book has helped you with your eBay business and you would like to know more, why not sign up for my weekly newsletter and keep up-to-date with the latest developments for eBay sellers. You can also send me your feedback and tell me how this book has kick-started your eBay adventure.

Distributed by the publisher of this book – Harriman House – each e-mail contains hints and tips for eBay sellers, technical developments within eBay, a reader's letter ('Ask Molly') and other essential information. HTML issues are also covered, with explanations of when and how to use additional codes to drive your profits even higher. Plus, check out new ideas surrounding general sales techniques and advice for moving with the markets.

It's not all hard work and no play. There are always strange and crazy things happening on eBay and in my 'Trader's Tales' section, I will share some of the more amusing moments from the world of sales. Like the guy who bought 'half a kilo of Lego' and then was disappointed with the amount! Not to mention the weird and wonderful auctions that take place online - how much would you bid for an 'air guitar'?

You can also keep up-to-date with my own eBay career; I'll share my experiences, both good and bad, with you.

To sign up to my free newsletter, please visit: www.ebaybulletin.co.uk

Best wishes,

Bob (Mollybol)

Harriman House
www.harriman-house.com

Tel: +44 (0)1730 233870 Fax: +44 (0)1730 233880
Email: contact@harriman-house.com
Harriman House Ltd, 3A Penns Road, Petersfield, Hampshire GU32 2EW UK